q739.27   99925

Jewelry

DATE DUE	
MAY 1 7 1995	5/08/02
JUL 0 8 1995	SEP 2 8 2004
AUG 0 8 1995	JAN 0 3 2005
MAR 0 8 1997	FEB 1 6 2006
APR 0 1 1997	
SEP 0 2 1997	
SEP 3 0 1997	
MAY 3 0 1998	
FEB 0 3 1999	
FEB 1 9 2000	
AUG 1 1 2000	
MAR 2 8 2001	
OCT 1 2 2001	
NOV 2 4 2001	
FEB 2 0 2002	
3/10/02	
APR 2 3 2002	
GAYLORD	PRINTED IN U.S.A.

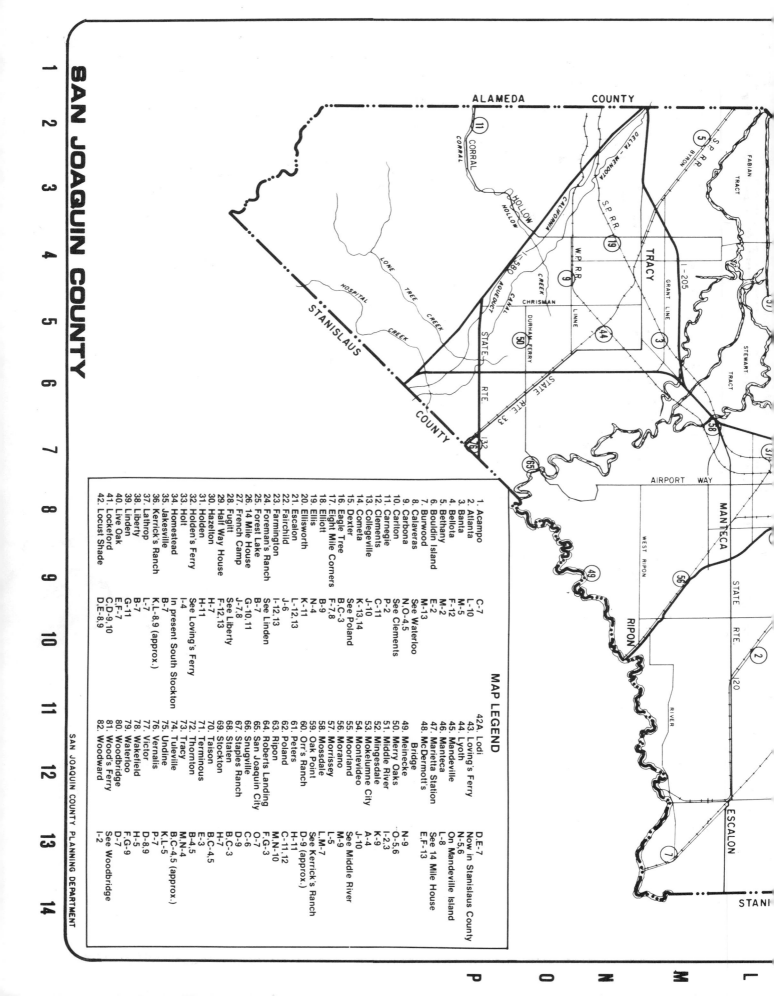

SAN JOAQUIN COUNTY

MAP LEGEND

#	Place	Location
1	Acampo	C-7
2	Atlanta	L-10
3	Banta	M-5
4	Bellota	F-12
5	Bethany	M-2
6	Bouldin Island	E-2
7	Burwood	M-13
8	Calaveras	See Waterloo
9	Carbona	N,O-4,5
10	Carlton	See Clements
11	Carnegie	P-2
12	Clements	C-11
13	Collegeville	J-10
14	Cometa	K-13,14
15	Dexter	See Poland
16	Eagle Tree	B,C-3
17	Eight Mile Corners	F-7,8
18	Elliott	B-9
19	Ellis	N-4
20	Ellsworth	K-11
21	Escalon	L-12,13
22	Fairchild	J-6
23	Farmington	I-12,13
24	Foreman's Ranch	See Linden
25	Forest Lake	B-7
26	14 Mile House	G-10,11
27	French Camp	J-7,8
28	Fugitt	See Liberty
29	Half Way House	F-12,13
30	Hazelton	H-7
31	Holden	H-11
32	Holden's Ferry	See Loving's Ferry
33	Holt	I-4
34	Homestead	In present South Stockton
35	Jakesville	B-7
36	Kerrick's Ranch	K,L-8,9 (approx.)
37	Lathrop	L-7
38	Liberty	B-7
39	Linden	G-11
40	Live Oak	E,F-7
41	Lockeford	C,D-9,10
42	Locust Shade	D,E-8,9
42A	Lodi	D,E-7
43	Loving's Ferry	Now in Stanislaus County
44	Lyoth	N-5,6
45	Mandeville	On Mandeville Island
46	Manteca	L-8
47	Marietta Station	See 14 Mile House
48	McDermott's Bridge	E,F-13
49	Meinecke	N-9
50	Merry Oaks	N,O-5,6
51	Middle River	I-2,3
52	Mingesdale	K-9
53	Mokelumne City	A-4
54	Montevideo	J-10
55	Moorland	See Middle River
56	Morano	M-9
57	Morrissey	L-5
58	Mossdale	L,M-7
59	Oak Point	See Kerrick's Ranch
60	Orr's Ranch	D-9 (approx.)
61	Peters	H-11
62	Poland	C-11,12
63	Ripon	M,N-10
64	Roberts Landing	F,G-3
65	San Joaquin City	O-7
66	Snugville	C-6
67	Staples Ranch	D-9
68	Staten	B,C-3
69	Stockton	H-7
70	Taison	B,C-4,5
71	Terminous	E-3
72	Thornton	B-4,5
73	Tracy	M,N-4
74	Tuleville	B,C-4,5 (approx.)
75	Undine	K,L-5
76	Vernalis	P-7
77	Victor	D-8,9
78	Wakefield	H-5
79	Waterloo	F,G-9
80	Woodbridge	D-7
81	Wood's Ferry	See Woodbridge
82	Woodward	I-2

HART PICTURE ARCHIVES

Jewelry

Under the General Editorship of
Harold H. Hart

Text by Nancy Goldberg

Hart Publishing Company, Inc. • New York City

COPYRIGHT © 1977, HART PUBLISHING COMPANY, INC.
NEW YORK, NEW YORK 10012

ISBN NO. 08055-1210-1 (PAPERBACK 08055-0303-X)
LIBRARY OF CONGRESS CATALOG CARD NO. 76-54049

MANUFACTURED IN THE UNITED STATES OF AMERICA

CONTENTS

HOW TO USE THIS BOOK   5

The History of Jewelry   6
Amulets   14
Armbands   16
Belts, Buckles, & Clasps   18
Bracelets   22
Brooches & Pins   34
Cameos   56
Chains   62
Crosses   68
Crowns & Tiaras   72

Earrings   76
Hair Ornaments & Combs   86
Medallions   90
Miscellaneous Jewelry   96
Necklaces   102
Pendants   116
Rings   128
Watches   134

SOURCES   142
INDEX   143

HOW TO USE THIS BOOK

JEWELRY is a collection of over 1,000 pictures of many periods culled from 27 known sources. These pictures have been subdivided into 17 categories.

All these pictures are in the public domain. They derive from magazines, books, and pictures copyrighted by Hart Publishing Company, now released to the public for general use.

So as not to clutter a caption, the source is given an abbreviated designation. Full publication data may be found in the *Sources* section, in which all sources are listed in alphabetical order, with the full title of the book or magazine, the publisher, and the date of publication. The *Sources* section commences on page 142.

Thirty-four of the pictures are halftones, and are designated by a square symbol □ at the end of the caption. These pictures, too, are suitable for reproduction, but the user is alerted to rescreen such a picture or convert it into line. All other pictures can be reproduced directly in line.

This volume contains an index, which begins on page 143. All index entries set in full caps represent one of the 17 major groupings in this book.

The History of Jewelry

In every era, every geographic location, and among every race or tribe of people since the dawn of history, jewelry has held an almost mystic attraction for mankind. Adornments of gems, metals, and other materials have played an important part in every civilization known to historians; no culture has ever been so rude as not to consider ornamentation an important feature in the beautification of the human body.

Of course, the characteristics of jewelry have varied widely among different types of cultures through the ages. Materials used to make jewelry have varied from seeds and nuts to precious gems. Styles of jewelry include complex, many-colored, gem-studded ornaments as well as simple, unadorned blocks or bits of metal. But no matter what its elements or its style, jewelry has always held a significance for man that transcends its economic value or even its worth in enhancing the beauty of the wearer. This reverence can be seen today in our own language, in such expressions as "Diamonds are a girl's best friend," or "She is an absolute *jewel*," referring to a person one has great affection or respect for.

Why this special feeling for bits of metal, stone, and even seeds or shells? Philosophers and historians have several theories to explain this phenomenon. First, there is our fascination with its durability; we know that our jewels will long outlive us. The jewels we own may someday be a record of our existence, our way of life, our tastes and preferences, and perhaps ultimately of our importance.

In addition, as a species infatuated with our bodies and devoted to their beautification and adornment, we value jewelry for its ability to enhance that beauty in our own and others' eyes.

Our preoccupation with an elusive ideal of perfection may also play a part in our reverence for lovely stones. A sparkling diamond, flashing all the colors of the rainbow with every slight movement, is clearly one of nature's more perfect creations.

There is, of course, a practical side to our enchantment with jewelry: the scarcity of many of the gems we adorn ourselves with, and hence their tremendous monetary value, has transformed some kinds of jewelry into symbols of rank, wealth, and social standing. In the same way as middle-class Americans value certain makes of

cars, the rich and nearly rich have always used their jewels as a statement of their economic and social status.

Another economic advantage of jewelry is its easy convertibility into cash—no mean virtue in a time of economic instability or among a people who are unsure of their security. East European Jews, for example, who lived under the constant threat of persecution, cherished their jewels for this reason.

Finally, the common use of jewels in the rituals and magical ceremonies of primitive peoples has led some historians to believe that gems were the focal point of early man's development of aesthetic feeling. The love of beauty, so universal to mankind, may have derived from the love of jewels.

Sources for the Study of Jewelry

Unfortunately, the very popularity of jewelry and the tremendous variation in its significance to man have hindered our ability to study it. Until the nineteenth century, antique jewelry was not thought to be of especially great value. Shifts in taste and style, as opposed to the monetary value of the gems themselves, caused most stones to be lifted from their original settings, sometimes many times over, in order to be placed in more contemporary and "stylish" settings. The old settings were normally discarded or melted down to make new ones.

Thus, only rarely has a piece of jewelry been preserved in its original form. For the most part, these unique specimens belong to private collections, where they are unavailable for viewing, and museums. Although some museums have excellent collections and are extremely important to the study of jewelry, the disadvantages of museums for the researcher are very real: the pieces are isolated in glass display cases, stripped of their primary function, and unavailable for handling except by a privileged few. Since the only reason a particular ornament has survived in its original form may be its mediocrity, the extant pieces may indeed be a lopsided representation of the originals.

It is for this reason that portraits have come to be of great importance to the study of jewelry. Some of these portraits (which begin to be relevant for their detail in the second half of the fifteenth century) meticulously portray the most ostentatious and valuable jewels ever designed. It is said, for example, that a goldsmith was employed for an entire month on the gem-studded collar for the effigy of Ferdinand of Portugal at Innsbruck. Portraits also illustrate the relationship of the jewelry of an era to that era's style of dress and hair. For instance, the elaborate necklaces and pendants of the Renaissance, constructed of gold, enamel, emeralds, rubies, and sapphires, can only be fully appreciated when seen against the background of the heavily brocaded, brightly colored costumes of the time. The pink- and yellow-tinted diamonds popular in the time of Louis XV and Louis XVI are immeasurably enhanced when placed against the lively pastel-colored clothing worn during those reigns.

Apart from the jewels in private and museum collections and those rendered in portraits and on statues, we have several other sources for our study of the history of jewelry. Much can be learned from the surviving designs for jewels. Painted in the margins of the fifteenth-century Books of Hours, are many beautiful examples of jewelry. A significant number of drawings also survives from the sixteenth century, and many engraved designs dating from the late fifteenth century to the end of the nineteenth have been discovered. The practice of making half-tone plates (several of which are included in this volume) originated in Paris, but this is a fairly recent development.

Another valuable, albeit less vivid, source is documentary. Bills, inventories, literary references to particular jewels, and especially advertisements survive from many of the later periods in the development of jewelry. It is from these documents that we perceive trends, both in styles and in the availability of jewelry to most people.

The Spread of Fine Jewelry to the Middle Classes

For a very long time, precious stones were the privilege of only a small minority. Indeed, from the thirteenth century to the late eighteenth century, the right to wear jewelry was often restricted by law to a nation's royalty or its very rich. An edict promulgated in France in 1283 prohibited citizens from wearing precious stones, pearls, and particular kinds of gold and silver jewelry; similar laws, some even more severe, were promulgated in Spain and in England. As late as 1720 in France, the wearing of pearls, diamonds, and other gems was forbidden.

The difficulty of enforcing these edicts is evidence of the mysterious power jewelry holds for man. Legend has it that King Henry IV's decree forbidding the wearing of gold and jewels in his kingdom was totally ignored by his subjects. The king thus found it necessary to construct an auxiliary law to the effect that only thieves and prostitutes were exempt from the ruling. Only then did all evidence of jewelry disappear from view.

Towards the end of the eighteenth century, with the development of the middle-class and its growing social and economic power in Europe, the wearing of fine jewelry had begun to spread. Of course, folk jewelry, constructed of semi-precious and relatively valueless jewels, had always been common, but by the middle of the nineteenth century, even fine jewelry—though not as grand as the jewelry belonging to the rich—was worn by nearly everyone. This factor, along with the innovation of mass production, has influenced the styles and trends in the making of jewelry up to the present day.

Ancient Jewelry

The use of jewelry is thought to antedate the use of clothing in early recorded history. According to surviving documents, the ornaments of primitive peoples were constructed of such varied elements as berries, seeds, nuts, perforated stones, feathers, bones, teeth, shells, ivory, and metals such as bronze, silver, and gold.

Several ancient periods stand out for their unique characteristics and beauty of design. The tombs of ancient Egypt have been particularly rich in discoveries. In 1894-1895, J. de Morgan excavated at Dahshur the tombs of five princesses of the Twelfth dynasty (2400 B.C.), which yielded an incredible series of finds.

Even at this early date, the work of ancient Egyptian jewelers was sophisticated and accurate. The Egyptians were adept at all kinds of jewel work, including chiseling, soldering, inlaying with colored stones, molding, and working with twisted wires and filigree (a decorative technique employing grains, beads, and fine wire of gold, silver or copper in intricate and delicate patterns). The first known evidence of granulated work—tiny grains of gold soldered on a smooth surface—was also found in the Egyptian collection.

Another remarkable collection of jewelry was discovered in the coffin of Queen Aah-hotp, who lived nearly a thousand years after the five princesses of the Twelfth dynasty. Though rougher and more coarse than the earlier collection, this assortment exhibits its designers' ingenuity and their masterful use of materials. The handiwork includes hammered work, incised or chased work (a process in which metal is indented with a hammer or other instrument without a cutting edge), soldering, combinations of layers of gold plates, and inlaying with colored stones.

The gold ornaments discovered around 1876 by Heinrich Schliemann in the graves of Mycenae, in Greece, have matched in brilliance and sophistication everything that has been known and theorized about the splendor of Mycenaean civilization, which reached its peak between 1400 and 1200 B.C. A wide range of personal ornaments were found: necklaces with gold beading and pendants, detailed butterflies, single and concentric circles, rosettes and leafage, crosses and stars constructed of combined crosses. The spiral, formed by means of twisted gold wires, was a common decoration. Grasshoppers or tree crickets in gold relief, made by hammering or pressing on the reverse side (a process known as repoussé), were also prevalent. In addition, pinheads and brooches were found—their heads ornamented in gold with the heads and bodies of various animals, and with silver blades or pointed pins inserted so that the ornament could be attached to clothing.

At Hissarlik, the supposed site of Troy, Schliemann discovered a great wealth of jewelry. His finds were of two general categories—one characterized by the same spirals and rosettes found at Mycenae, and the other, larger category composed of less sophisticated artifacts, including diadems (ornamental headbands), earrings, beads, and bracelets. These latter objects were probably the products of a local and uncultured art.

The Mycenaean-type group was composed mainly of gold necklaces, brooches, bracelets, hair-pins, earrings, beads, and twisted wire drops. Spirals of twisted wire and small rosettes with tiny stones set into the centers appear in abundance throughout. Some of the more sophisticated ornaments, however, bear little or no relation to those at Mycenae. These include diadems of pure hammered gold cut into thin plates, which were attached to rings by double gold wires and fastened together at the back with thin twisted wire. These gold plates and rings hung from a headband in long strips across the forehead, with even longer strips hanging at each side of the face close to the temples. This type of ornament was presumably worn exclusively by women.

Mycenaean influence also extended to the jewelry found in the cemetery at Enkomi near Salamis, in Cyprus. Indeed, this jewelry is probably the best representation we have of the close of the Mycenaean period. Its geometric patterns are entirely Mycenaean in nature, although its forms—representations of mythical figures, such as the sphinx and the griffin—were apparently inherited from archaic Greek art. The tombs contain all forms of jewelry, with heavy emphasis on pins, rings, and diadems with patterns in relief. The Enkomi finds are not unique; jewelry exhibiting archaic Greek themes and figures set into typical Mycenaean geometric patterns in gold has been discovered elsewhere in that region.

Unfortunately, the search for examples of ancient Assyrian jewelry has met with little success. We do, however, have a sense of the distinct character of Assyrian jewelry from other sources. Bas-reliefs, dating from the ninth to the seventh centuries B.C., provide magnificent evidence of the Assyrians' use of personal decoration. Representations of jewels such as bracelets, necklaces, and earrings, which were probably constructed of precious metals, have been gathered from these bas-reliefs; in one, Assur-nazir-pal, king of Assyria from 885 to 860 B.C., is shown wearing a cross which bears a striking resemblance to the Maltese cross of modern times.

Greek, Etruscan, and Roman Jewelry

Decorative art from the beginning of the classical Greek period is represented by the discoveries of the archeologist G. D. Hogarth. In 1905, Hogarth unearthed nearly 1000 gold ornaments, packed closely together, which had been buried in the soil beneath the central basis of the temple of Artemis at Ephesus. They appear to date back to the seventh or sixth century B.C., and were probably a ritual offering to Artemis, the earth goddess. The collection is particularly rich in pins, brooches, beads, and stamped gold disks.

The evidence indicates that the Greeks were expert goldsmiths; their early work is characterized by exquisitely wrought gold work unadorned with stones or other color. After 400 B.C., Greek craftsmen began to set precious stones in gold. This was followed by work with cameos—a style which was later enthusiastically imitated by the Romans.

Greek, Etruscan, and Roman jewelry are strikingly similar in nature. Fretwork (an ornamental net of interwoven metal) is common to the jewelry of all three, as are the wave ornament, the guilloche (interlacing curved lines), and the use of the human figure. The goldsmiths' work is so intricate and so fine that it can hardly be duplicated by modern craftsmen. The purest examples of this work have been derived from the tombs of Kerch and the Crimea, and are currently housed at the Hermitage.

Etruscan jewelry (from the area of what is now called Tuscany in Italy), reached its peak between the seventh and fifth centuries B.C. It is largely indistinguishable from Greek jewelry, although its later forms are slightly more diffuse and florid than the Greek forms, with less precision of design. The art of granulation as practiced by the Etruscan goldsmiths, however, reached a remarkable stage of refinement. Indeed, later craftsmen were mystified by the technique and unable to duplicate it until the latter part of the nineteenth century, when Castellani of Rome discovered goldworkers in the Abruzzi region of Italy to whom the intricate process had been passed down from one generation to another. He persuaded some of these men to come to Naples in order to teach other goldsmiths, and thus succeeded in reviving the lost art. Examples of this rediscovered process were exhibited at the London Exhibition of 1872.

Roman jewelry was based predominantly on Greek and Etruscan forms, but as a rule it was much larger, with many surfaces of plain and undecorated metal. Sometimes gold coins of the realm were adapted for use as earrings or pendants. The later Romans apparently valued their jewelry more for its precious stones and cameos than for originality or skill of setting. Cameos, ropes of pearls, and flat gold surfaces set with many huge, brilliantly colored stones were characteristic of that era.

The Post-Roman Era

The jewelry of the post-Roman period can be divided into two general categories. One developed with the approach of the barbarian tribes, and is known as the Teutonic style. Coarse and primitive, jewelry of this style depicted conventionalized animal forms such as clumsy horse-headed brooches and bird-shaped fibulae. Gilt bronze and occasionally gold were the most common elements. Stones were often cut to special shapes to be inlaid into perforated gold plates. Jewelry of this type has been found over a wide field ranging from Siberian tombs to Spain, with minor differentiating local characteristics.

The second, more refined artifacts of the post-Roman period are commonly known as Merovingian jewelry and date from the fifth century B.C. This type is characterized by thin plates of gold decorated with enamel, poured into divided areas in a design outlined with bent wire fillets or metal strips, which were then soldered into a gold background—a procedure known as cloisonné. Thin slabs of garnet were also used, and some pieces have decorative details of filigree work, beading, and twisted gold reminiscent of the traditions of previous civilizations.

In countries where both forms of jewelry can be found, a certain class distinction can be theorized about their use. The Greek, Etruscan, and Roman techniques incorporated into the more refined jewelry seem to have been limited to the tastes of the ruling class; whereas the Teutonic forms of gilt bronze belonged to the ruled. The evolution of jewelry can be seen as paralleling the development of an ever more civilized culture, with the rulers (or tribal leaders) naturally adjusting their tastes more quickly to subtler and more intricate forms of art. Progress in both jewelry design and in civilization occurred through the gradual victory of the more refined methods over the more primitive ones.

Celtic Jewelry

The Celts, a group of tribes who dominated Central Europe in the second millennium B.C. (and who could be found throughout Western Europe as late as the fourth century B.C.) progressed through a long independent evolution in jewelry-making. In its early stages, during the mid-European Iron Age, Celtic jewel work is particularly notable for its combinations of curves, with strange thickenings in the center of the design which give the art a quasi-naturalistic effect. The Celts' decorative craft work included a skillful use of inlaid enamel and chased work. In the period after the introduction of Christianity, Western European jewelry, deriving from the Celts' early work, featured interlaced winding scrolls and other new forms of decoration added to the older traditions. This gradually evolved toward the extreme complexity of early Irish illumination (decoration with gold, silver, or brilliant colors, or with designs or miniature pictures) and metal work. The characteristic Celtic ornaments of the earlier period—hammered work with details in repoussé, inlaid with vitreous paste, colored enamel, and amber—are in the later stages embellished with rock crystal, which had a smooth rounded surface, and with the characteristic winding scrolls.

Byzantium

The Byzantine empire, centered in Constantinople after the introduction of Christianity, stretched throughout the entire Mediterranean area and into parts of the

East and Europe. Byzantine art generally provided a transition between earlier techniques and those of the medieval period to come—and the art of making jewelry was no exception. Lavish in color and design, Byzantine jewelry descended from composite Greek and Roman styles, but it incorporated many features of Eastern technique and eventually some European characteristics. In its most glorious period, under the rule of Justinian I and Theodora (527-65 A.D.), a revival of Hellenism led to a rebirth of many of the techniques which had been lost since the period of Greek domination.

The Medieval Period and the Early Renaissance

Jewelry in the Middle Ages (from the tenth to the thirteenth centuries) was generally simple but massive; large rings, brooches, and girdles predominated. Amber beads were usually set into the pieces, probably to ward off evil spirits. By 1300, amber had been largely replaced by glass.

During the Renaissance, which emerged in Italy in the fourteenth century, individual expression and cultural achievement acquired a new and unprecedented importance. Jewelry design experienced a rapid transformation: noted artists and even architects designed and rendered pieces of jewelry. The results were the triumphs of Albrecht Dürer, Benvenuto Cellini, and Hans Holbein. Particularly in Italy, goldsmiths consistently produced work of surpassing excellence. Gorgeous jewelry encrusted with enamel and precious stones— necklaces with pendants, jewelled collars, brooches, heavy gold link chains—was worn by both men and women. The art of engraving reached new heights, producing skillful representations of human and animal figures, and the process of incising such designs with niello (a metallic alloy with a deep black color) achieved an excellence of quality and aesthetic beauty which has never been rivaled.

The Seventeenth to the Mid-Nineteenth Centuries

Towards the end of the Renaissance, the fascination with gems had grown to enormous proportions; design and setting were no longer of paramount importance. By the late seventeenth century, the art of the goldsmith and enameler—and their prestige—had given way to that of the lapidary (gem-cutter) and mounter. Brilliant effects were attempted by massing the gold, or by placing the stones in elaborate clusters of various shapes.

The result was a hodgepodge which looked as if as many valuable stones as possible had been squeezed into a given space. Rather than achieving a harmonious balance between gems and metal, craftsmen obtained a merely mechanical excellence—an ornate and excessive interpretation of tradition with nothing original or beautiful about it. The exquisite traditions of Oriental jewelry, which had been passed down in some form throughout all the periods described above, were now comparatively lost. In the London Exhibition of 1851, Europe's loss was obvious in the Oriental examples contributed by India; in their simplicity and subtlety, the Oriental pieces put to shame the extravagances of their European counterparts.

An exhibition in Paris, arranged by Castellani in 1867, displayed a remarkable collection of European jewelry of a different nature. This was an assortment of peasant jewelry, the traditional ornaments of the common peoples of France (chiefly Normandy), Spain, Holland, Denmark, Portugal, Germany, and Switzerland. This fascinating collection, now in the Victoria and Albert Museum, indicates that the forms popular in one country are often followed and adapted in others, almost always because of the perfection of their design for practical use.

Apart from these humbler branches of the art, which have always flourished in every period of history, the period of the seventeenth through the mid-nineteenth centuries saw little in the way of innovation or beauty. In 1680, a method was discovered for making imitation pearls, which precipitated the popularity of ropes of pearls for women. In the late eighteenth century, the new popularity of decorative buttons, watches, and snuff boxes almost superceded the wearing of jewelry. After 1800, however, the bracelet, which had nearly disappeared with the style of cuffed and ruffed long sleeves, became prominent once more. The early nineteenth century also saw the revival of the cameo as an ornament, and new forms of decoration were introduced, such as the watch and chain, and matching sets of jewelry.

The Mid-Nineteenth and Early Twentieth Centuries

Apart from these few innovations and revivals, jewelry-making remained virtually a lost art until nearly the end of the nineteenth century. In the last quarter of the century, particularly in Paris, a new artistic mode managed to break away from the stale, poorly maintained traditions of earlier periods.

The first evidence of a new era was provided at the Paris Exhibition of 1878, with the art of a designer named Massin. This skillful artist and craftsman produced light pierced designs whose form was borrowed from natural flowers. With his introduction of this fresh element, and with his particular use of gold filigree, Massin created a new style of jewelry design.

Also during this period, the arts of setting and design regained their importance. New discoveries of gem deposits in South Africa in the late 1860s and 1870s—which caused a drop in the value of diamonds and other precious stones—were partially responsible for this trend. Until this time, the enormous value of the stones themselves had been the jeweler's chief consideration in designing his ornaments; a setting was important only insofar as it displayed the stone to its best advantage. Settings themselves often fell victim to the whims of fashion, so that only rarely was a gem preserved in its original setting. The jeweler's awareness of the impermanence of his work was obviously not conducive to a truly artistic or careful effort.

As diamonds and other gems fell in value, much of their prestige was lost. This factor encouraged the rebirth of interest in simple gold and silver. People were more willing to value a piece of jewelry for its delicacy of design or skillful finish, whether or not the piece was studded with precious stones.

This shift in decorative tastes, which developed slowly at first, reached revolutionary proportions in the Salon of 1895 in Paris. With an unprecedented power and effect, the designs of René Lalique burst upon the art world. Only five years later, at the exhibition of 1900, Lalique's enormous influence became obvious in the imitations and adaptations of his work by many other craftsmen.

Lalique's major contribution to the art of jewelry design was his originality—his refusal to adhere to any preconceived notions of how an ornament must be designed. He formulated his own principles, discarding many of the traditions which had bound jewelers for centuries to a monotonous, moribund school of design. He drew freely from nature and from the past—the art of Egypt, Greece, and the Orient—but with new elements of design which added fresh feeling to the old structures. His soft double curves, delicate floral forms, and iridescent harmonies of coloring combined the crafts of the goldsmith, the chaser, the enameler, and the gem-setter, giving each a new spirit by freeing it from the narrow structure to which it had been confined.

Lalique's most striking revolt against the traditional laws of the trade was his refusal to acknowledge the hierarchy of gems; he believed the stones themselves were subordinate to the structure of the design and to their appropriateness for a particular piece of work. Thus, while he would sometimes use precious stones such as emeralds, rubies, sapphires, or even diamonds as backgrounds, he would often leave the conspicuous center place for a stone of little value, such as carnelian, agate, malachite, jasper, or coral. Indeed, Lalique sometimes used common materials, such as horn, which had never before held a place in the jeweler's art. The opal, with its milky, iridescent, translucent color, lent itself well to Lalique's arrangements of color. One of his favorite stones, the opal quickly became all the rage in France.

Although Lalique's striking originality provided a needed freshness to the art of jewelry design, it was finally not very practical. For many social and psychological reasons, the economic value of a jewel is inevitably tied to the corresponding personal value of that jewel for the wearer. For the great majority, a jewel which, though valuable for its beauty, was not valuable for the quality or rarity of its stones, could not hold its popularity or prestige forever, especially given the constantly changing moods of fashion. In addition, the critics of Lalique's work have pointed out that the products of his school were often impractical for normal wear and tear.

Nevertheless, Lalique's movement quickly spread to other countries, culminating in the excellent, fanciful designs of Alfred Gilbert and George J. Frampton of England, L.C. Tiffany in the United States and Philippe Wolfers in Belgium. Wolfers' designs, though heavier in style, were finely executed and singularly graceful, earning him the appropriate nickname "the Belgian Lalique."

Other countries whose craftsmen manifested some evidence of Lalique's influence were Germany, Austria, Russia, and Switzerland; most of the products of these nations, however, did not achieve the quality of lightness together with durability so essential to the practical use of the ornament, and which was one of the most brilliant achievements of the Italian Renaissance pieces. Thus, many of these creations are more beautiful in the box or display case than on the wearer.

The Twentieth Century—Modern Jewelry

Today, the greatest influence on the evolution of jewelry is the innovation of mass production. Of course, even in modern times, the evolution of handmade jewelry continues.

The European cities of Paris, Vienna, London, and Birmingham were the chief centers for the gradual development of mass-produced jewelry. Traditionally, jewelry-making methods depended entirely on the skill of the craftsman. Eventually certain procedures were invented—such as stamping various designs into the soft metal—which could assure exact duplication and symmetry in the designs which were repeated within a single piece. As early as 1872, a jeweler named Beltête, who suffered from rheumatism in his fingers, had invented such a mechanical device for cutting out and stamping settings.

These little conveniences were the amorphous beginnings of the age of mass-produced jewelry. As time passed, more and more of these labor-saving devices were introduced until finally came the establishment of large factories in which every step is accomplished by machine. Only a few finishing touches, or the fitting together of the pieces by hand, are necessary to form the finished product. Since much of the jewelry produced in the twentieth century has involved both mass production and handmaking techniques to some degree, it is difficult to draw a distinct line between them, except when the work is done exclusively by hand, or at the other extreme, when the entire piece is stamped out by automated processes and barely touched by human hands.

Whether it be handmade or manufactured, modern jewelry may be divided into three categories: those pieces in which the major design is formed by stones, with the metal base serving only as a background; those in which the gold or other metal, embellished by engraving, enameling, or other processes, plays at least as important a part as do the stones; and those in which the unadorned gold, silver, or platinum (a twentieth-century innovation) is itself the sole decoration. This last category is most likely to be manufactured rather than handmade; for example, almost every style of gold chain is now manufactured, because the intricacy of design and perfection of workmanship simply cannot be duplicated by hand.

The Production of Handmade Jewelry

The long, complicated process of designing and producing a piece of handmade jewelry begins with a drawing, usually in pencil, sepia, or watercolor. The craftsman's job is to reproduce, as precisely as possible, the design he has been given. According to the design, he hammers, cuts out, files and shapes the metal which forms the base of the work. Upon this base, he next solders (or sometimes rivets) whatever ornamentation is required. These ornaments—which may be representations of human and animal figures, flowers, leaves, or fruit—are first modeled in wax, then molded and cast in gold or other metal, and finally chased and finished. Since the metal becomes brittle through hammering and other work, it must be softened by passing it through a fire so that it can be more easily shaped. With elaborate procedures—repoussé, for example—after the general forms are shaped the interior is filled with a resinous compound which forms a solid but pliable body underneath the metal, allowing the final details to be wrought on the front of the design. Chasing is the final step in finishing the piece.

When stones are to be set into the piece, the metal must be carefully shaped by hand into tiny depressions, or cups, which will contain the stone. The edges of these cups are raised slightly above the surface of the base, then folded over the edges of the stone to secure it (in the making of fine jewelry, cement is never used).

Gem cutting is one of the most difficult and important aspects of the entire craft of jewelry-making. The way a stone is cut dramatically affects the brilliance, beauty, and general quality of the gem. Even the most perfect diamond can be reduced to a dull, inferior quality if cut at the wrong angle. The same is true of the angle at which a gem is set; stones set carelessly, however brilliant they may actually be, will appear quite ordinary in comparison with poorer stones which have been skillfully set.

The disadvantages of totally handmade jewelry are obvious. The tremendous amount of time required to create a single piece results in rather prohibitive costs, especially when the raw materials are expensive to begin with. Another disadvantage is the impossibility of attaining perfect symmetry within the piece, although many consider this characteristic of handmade jewelry as part of its beauty.

The Process of Mass-Producing Jewelry

Although machine-made jewelry begins the same way as handmade jewelry—with a design sketched or painted by an artist—there the similarity ends. From the design, steel dies are sunk, which stamp out as rapidly as possible from a plate of rolled metal the part of the design represented by each die. The only real skill required is that of the original designer of the steel dies, since from then on the process is entirely mechanized, requiring human hands only to fit the separate pieces together. Brooches, necklaces, bracelets, earrings, lockets are all struck out by the gross. This process eliminates the cost and time factors, as well as the problem of attaining perfect symmetry within a piece. We now have perfect duplication, even among thousands of pieces of jewelry.

Cost is determined solely by the value of the components; the quality and type of gem or metal sets the price. The quality of metal is determined by its proportion to the alloy it is combined with. Although 24-carat gold is pure gold, 18-carat gold is considered best for making chains; gold of higher proportions is too soft to keep the shape of the piece.

The lack of uniqueness in a piece of manufactured jewelry is counterbalanced for many people by its availability in terms of cost. The process has also made feasible the production of imitation, or "costume," jewelry; indeed, some of the most original, simple, and artistic pieces are designed for the imitation jewelry market.

Of course, the anonymity inherent in the production of a piece of jewelry designed for mass production is not conducive to creative, original work; thus the art of jewelry design has for the most part fallen into decline.

The Future of Jewelry

With the growth of imitation jewelry, especially stones and pearls, with gold-plated backgrounds, it is logical to assume that our jewels will not have the same value, financially nor emotionally, for our descendants as our ancestors' pieces have had for us. One might argue that throughout history the ornaments of the common people and the middle class have never played an important part in the development of jewelry; only the fine jewelry of the very rich has had a significant influence. Then the situation today is not so different; the fine, handmade, creatively designed pieces, as always, will influence the tastes of our descendants. Of course, one cannot fail to recognize the dearth of fine jewelry being made today, especially in contrast to previous eras.

Tastes have indeed changed from those opulent ages which prescribed magnificent displays of jewels. More often than not, we consider these in bad taste. Few people today covet diamonds "as big as the Ritz," or other lavish gem-encrusted jewels. When such jewels are bought, they are generally considered investments rather than ornaments, and they are locked away in safe-deposit boxes to gather dust and increased monetary value.

The result, on a professional level, is the decline of an art form which in the past was painstakingly learned over a period of many years. Even after investing the time needed to learn the art, professional craftsmen often find themselves designing costume jewelry in marcasite.

However, a recent phenomenon has occurred in the development of jewelry which could bring about a revolution in the art. More than ever before, amateurs are trying their creative talents in designing and handmaking jewelry—with surprisingly fine results. Whether taken up as a hobby or for profit, this trend may prove to be the future of jewelry as a flourishing art once more.

One thing remains certain: standards of beauty, though they often change, are inherent and necessary to the nature of mankind. The art of ornamentation is one of our greatest proofs of this eternal quest.

NANCY GOLDBERG

Amulets

An amulet is any object which its wearer believes has the power to protect him from evil. Amulets against witchcraft, sickness, accident, and a multitude of other dangers have helped man deal with his fears. An amulet differs from an icon in that it supposedly has an inherent power in and of itself, while the icon is considered a manifestation of some other deity or force which works through the object symbolized by it.

Although an amulet is generally hung in a pendant around the neck, it can also be strapped to an arm or leg, or even hung on a wall or doorway to protect the household.

Amulets have been constructed out of just about everything. Stones, metals, and strips of parchment, with figures or legends inscribed upon them, are the most common materials used. Primitive peoples used gems, seeds, and certain herbs, as well as the teeth, claws, and other parts of animals, since these supposedly conferred the characteristics of the animal upon the wearer.

The makers of amulets are said to have taken great care to select the proper time for construction, making sure the stars and planets were in the right position in the sky and that other magic influences were propitious, so that any negative force which could destroy or weaken the amulet's power would be minimized.

All primitive peoples have made use of amulets. We have many examples of amulets—particularly scarabs—used by the Egyptians, and others representing the Greek and Roman eras. The dictates of Mosaic law, which prescribed that portions of the law be bound to the hands and arms, led to the widespread superstition among poorly educated Jews that these phylacteries, as they are called, had powers of their own. Traces of these superstitions also appear in early Christianity; a favorite symbol engraved on the charms of the early Christians was the fish.

Belief in the power of an object to prevent bad luck or to bring good luck has persisted through modern times. Even our own civilization is not immune to it, as is evidenced by the superstitious use by some people of the rabbit's foot, four-leaf clover, and horseshoe. Although modern man does not re-

gard these good luck charms as seriously as his ancestors did, they are nevertheless direct descendants of ancient amulets.

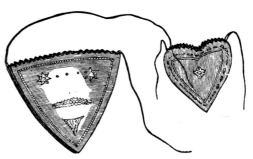

Ancient amulets. *L'Art Pour Tous, Vol. 9*

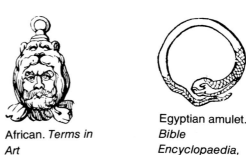

African. *Terms in Art*

Egyptian amulet. *Bible Encyclopaedia, Vol. 1*

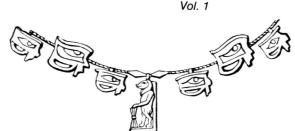

African. *Terms in Art*

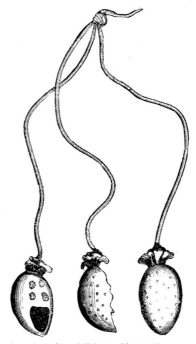

Amulets for children. *Natural History, Africa*

Scarab, from the
time of Thotmes
III. *Century Dictionary*

Ancient Egyptian amulet. *Land & Book, Vol. 1*

Egyptian scarab.
Connoisseur, Vol. 15

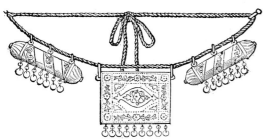

Ancient Egyptian amulet. *Land & Book, Vol. 1*

Egyptian scarab of faience and
stone, from the 26th Dynasty.
Connoisseur, Vol. 15

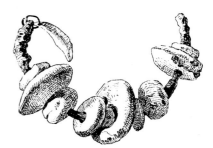

Ancient amulet constructed of stone.
L'Art Pour Tous, Vol. 9

Egyptian. *Bible
Encyclopaedia,
Vol. 1*

African. *Terms in
Art*

Egyptian. *Bible
Encyclopaedia,
Vol. 1*

Ancient Egyptican
amulet. *Terms in
Art*

Egyptian amulet.
*Bible
Encyclopaedia,
Vol. 1*

Egyptian scarab of steatite, from the 26th-30th Dynasties. *Connoisseur, Vol. 15*

Ancient Egyptian
amulet. *Terms in
Art*

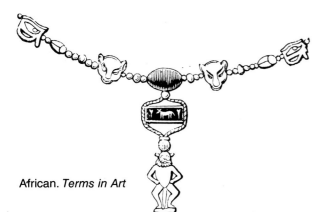

African. *Terms in Art*

Egyptian scarab.
Connoisseur, Vol. 15

Oriental amulet. *Terms in Art*

Armbands

The armband, a form of bracelet worn high on the arm, is one of the oldest known pieces of jewelry; examples have been found which were worn during the earliest days of ancient Egypt. Armbands were also worn by the ancient Medes and Persians. They are often mentioned in the Bible, apparently as ornaments for men as well as women.

Frequently made of gold and inlaid with precious stones, Egyptian armbands were usually painted in enamel. The many different colors and shades varied from bright hues to pale pastels.

In ancient Greece, armbands were fashioned out of every conceivable material, in a multitude of designs. Among the various types, the Greeks apparently preferred the spiral form, which is described in detail in Homer's *Iliad.* These spiral armbands often assumed the shape of snakes, which encircled the arm two, three, or even more times. Whatever form they took, armbands were worn exclusively by the women.

In contrast, among the ancient Italian tribes, the wearing of armbands was the exclusive prerogative of men. The Sabines, for example, often wore extremely heavy armbands on their left arms. During the Roman period, armbands were chiefly military decorations, bestowed by generals for acts of bravery or valor. Roman women of this period wore both bracelets (encircling the wrist) and armbands for personal decoration.

The ancient Germanic tribes apparently wore bracelets and armbands almost to the exclusion of all other forms of jewelry. Although these ornaments were worn by both men and women, the spiral armband was particularly favored by men, judging by the numerous examples found in their tombs.

Today, armbands are worn only rarely by the peoples of Western cultures. They are, however, still fairly common among the peoples of the Arab and Oriental nations.

Ancient Egyptian.
Iconographic

Ancient Greek.
Handbook of Ornament

Roman armband.
Iconographic

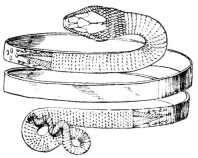

Assyrian armband.
Handbook of Ornament

Ancient Greek. *Handbook of Ornament*

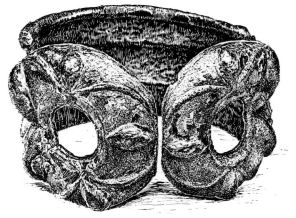

Armband of beaten bronze. *Illustrated London News*

Ancient Egyptian.
Sunday Book

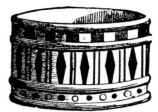

Ancient Egyptian.
Sunday Book

Ancient Egyptian.
Sunday Book

Ancient Egyptian.
Sunday Book

Ancient Egyptian.
Sunday Book

Persian. *Century
Dictionary*

Ancient Egyptian.
Sunday Book

Egyptian. *Century
Dictionary*

Ancient Egyptian.
Sunday Book

Ancient Egyptian.
Sunday Book

German. *The Workshop*

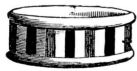

Ancient Egyptian.
Sunday Book

Ancient Egyptian.
Sunday Book

Gaulish armband, gold. *Illustrated
London News*

Belts, Buckles, and Clasps

In the Greek and Roman eras, emphasis was placed on the artistic design of buckles and clasps used as belt fasteners. By the post-Roman period, belt buckles had become an essential component of the warrior's costume and equipment; they were thus important considerations in the work of metalsmiths. Great care was taken with the intricate ornamentation of these buckles. The rich designs of the Germanic invaders, for example, often represented two or more wild animals locked in mortal struggle.

Belt buckles and clasps found in the graves of the Franks and Burgundians were often ornamented with chased or inlaid silver or bronze. A heavy rectangular buckle, found in the tomb of Childeric I, king of the Franks in the fifth century, was decorated in filigree. Examples from the seventh century show gold work with interlacing curvilinear patterns and cutaway tongues.

During the Middle Ages, the buckle took on an even higher degree of importance in the art of ornamentation. In the second half of the fourteenth century—the age of knights in shining armor—the decoration of belts and buckles reached its most splendid heights.

With the advent of the shoe buckle, the art reached a new stage of development during the reign of Louis XIV in France (1650-1715). For centuries in the history of Western civilization, jewelry had been the unique prerogative of women; the only adornment acceptable for men were finger rings, buttons, and belt buckles. By the end of the seventeenth century, men began to make the best of these restrictions by adorning themselves with buckles—not only on their belts, but also on their shoes, at their knees, and on their cuffs. Fashionable fops of the eighteenth century wore thin shoes adorned with huge buckles of gold, silver, and other precious metals. These were sometimes even set with real or imitation gems of paste and marcasite.

By the twentieth century, women had adopted this ornamental style as their own, and today, shoe buckles are more common on women's shoes than on men's. Belt buckles, for both sexes, continue to play a part in stylish attire. Many contemporary fashion designers also create these accessories as part of a total fashion look. Of course, as with other pieces of jewelry, the trend of today is toward simplicity and understatement.

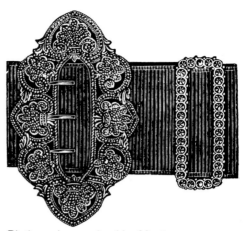

Platinum-bronze buckle. *Montgomery*

Clasp, manufactured by M. Froment-Meurice of Paris. *Industry of Nations*

Silver belt buckle. *Montgomery*

Art nouveau belt buckle. *Barnett* □

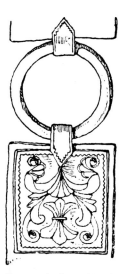

Bronze belt and buckle.
Handbook of Ornament

Silver belt buckle.
Montgomery

Norwegian silver clasps. *Simple Jewelry* □

Roman gold sash buckle with
turquoise. *Sears Catalogue*

Hanging chain of 16th century
French belt. *L'Art Pour Tous, Vol. 19*

Silver-trimmed belt of silk web.
Montgomery

Belt with chains. *L'Art Pour Tous, Vol. 9*

Belts, Buckles, & Clasps continued

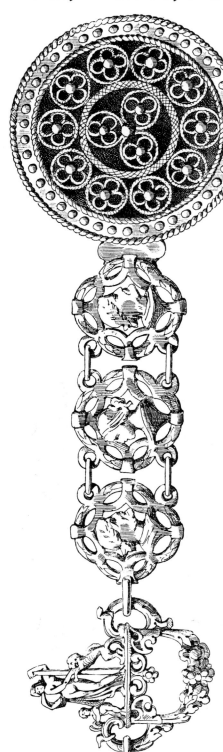

16th century French belt.
L'Art Pour Tous, Vol. 19

Gold plaque belt.
*L'Art Pour Tous,
Vol. 20*

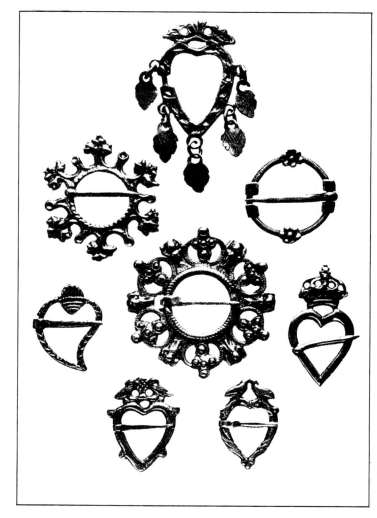

Norwegian silver betrothal clasps. *Simple Jewelry*

Clasp, manufactured by M.
Froment-Meurice of Paris. *Industry of
Nations*

Ladies' embossed leather belt.
Montgomery

Ladies' embossed leather belt.
Montgomery

Gold engraved belt. *L'Art Pour Tous, Vol. 20*

Belt and buckle. *Handbook of Ornament*

Etruscan belt. *L'Art Pour Tous, Vol. 3*

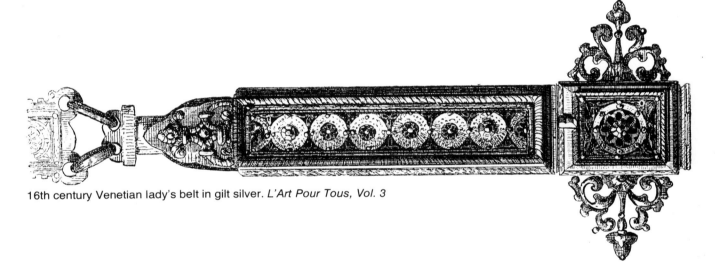

16th century Venetian lady's belt in gilt silver. *L'Art Pour Tous, Vol. 3*

16th century Venetian lady's belt in gilt silver. *L'Art Pour Tous, Vol. 3*

Silver-trimmed belt of silk web.
Montgomery

17th century Russian buckle.
L'Art Pour Tous, Vol. 41

Silver-trimmed belt of silk web.
Montgomery

Bracelets

From prehistoric times to the present, the bracelet has been a popular form of ornamentation. In the Bronze Age, bracelets were constructed mainly of gold and of bronze (silver was unknown at that time). They were oval or penannular in shape, with expanding—often trumpet-shaped—ends. While gold bracelets of this period were fashioned by un-adorned hammered work, bent into shape, the bronze work was often chased with decorative de-signs and patterns.

The Bible mentions three distinct types of bracelets, and although we cannot be sure of the dis-tinctive characteristics, we know that one type was worn exclusively by men, one by women, and one by either sex. The Egyptians wore bracelets of plain or enameled metal, unadorned by stones.

Greek and Assyrian bracelets fall into two general categories: one formed of coiled spirals, usually in the form of snakes; and the other formed of stiff penannular hoops, with rams' heads, lions' heads, or in some cases, enameled sphinxes, forming the two ends. In late Etruscan art, the bracelets were often formed of separate, connected panels, a style which is still in vogue today.

During Europe's Iron Age, the Greek spiral forms were common. Toward the close of the pagan period, plaited silver bracelets and designs of inter-twisted strands of silver wire became popular. The Celtic period saw the development of serpent-shaped bracelets and massive armlets which covered nearly the entire arm. Perhaps this was an adapta-tion of a German and Scandinavian technique com-mon in the Bronze Age, when it was used as protec-tion against sword attack rather than as personal decoration.

Among the Eastern cultures, bracelets are ex-tremely popular with women, who may wear several on the same wrist. All kinds of materials—including mother-of-pearl, gold, and silver for the finer quality bracelets and plated steel, horn, brass, copper, and beads for the more common folk jewelry—are em-ployed for construction. In China, bracelets are sometimes cut out of a single piece of jade.

For no other reason than a change in taste, the Middle Ages saw a decline in the popularity of bracelets throughout Europe. The Renaissance,

however, brought a renewal of interest in bracelets, as well as in other types of jewelry.

This popularity has remained alive to this day. Modern styles reflect the influences of virtually ev-ery period and style in history.

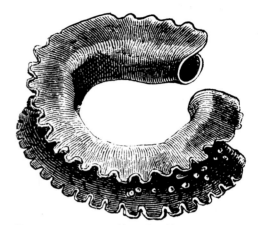

Egyptian. *Illustrated London News*

Assyrian silver bracelet.
St. Nicholas

Gold and enamel bracelet. *The Workshop, Vol. 8*

Bracelet set with pearl and diamond.
Illustrated London News

Renaissance style.
The Workshop, Vol. 7

Enamel bracelet with diamonds and emeralds, by Phillips Bros. of London. *Industry of Nations*

Fine ruby and diamond half-hoop.
Spiers

Gold bracelet set with pearls.
Spiers

16th century French. *L'Art Pour Tous, Vol. 19*

Designed by M. Froment-Meurice of Paris. *Industry of Nations*

Bracelets continued

Diamond cluster and scroll.
Spiers

Pearl double hearts. *Spiers*

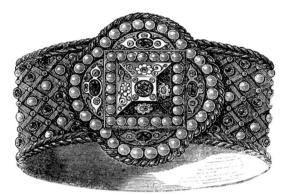

Bracelet given to Princess Helena
by the Maharajah Dhuleep Singh.
Illustrated London News

Diamond cluster and scrolls.
Spiers

Pearl flowers and leaves.
Spiers

Bracelet by G. Ehni. *The Workshop, Vol. 6*

Gold bracelet by von Demfelben of Germany. *The Workshop, Vol. 5*

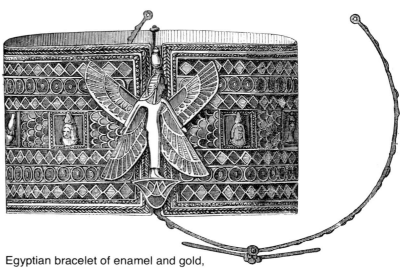

Egyptian bracelet of enamel and gold,
in the Munich Museum. *Industry of Nations*

African. *Natural History, Africa*

Curb and bead center.
Spiers

Renaissance style. *The Workshop, Vol. 7*

Designed by G. Ehni of Stuttgart, Germany, for export
into Havana and Mexico. *The Workshop, Vol. 2*

Blue and white enamel, by Phillips Bros. of London. *Industry of Nations*

Bracelets continued

Designed by G. Ehni of Stuttgart, Germany, for export
into Havannah and Mexico. *The Workshop, Vol. 2*

Renaissance style, from Germany. *The Workshop, Vol. 7*

Plaques of gold with corded ornaments, from the Louvre Museum. *History of Furniture*

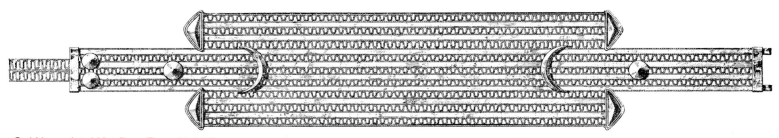

Gold bracelet. *L'Art Pour Tous, Vol. 20*

Enamel bracelet with diamonds, by C. Rowlands & Son of London. *Industry of Nations*

Bracelet set with diamonds and carbuncles, by S.H. & D. Gass of London. *Industry of Nations*

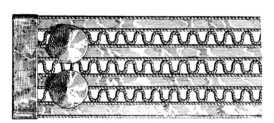

Clasp of gold bracelet. *L'Art Pour Tous, Vol. 20*

Primitive silver bracelet of Dinajpur, Bengal.
Industry of Nations

Pearl sprays. *Spiers*

Pearls, olivines, and diamonds. *Spiers*

Enamel and gold bracelet with diamonds and carbuncles,
by Martin, Baskett & Martin of Cheltenham, England. *Industry of Nations*

Bracelets continued

Designed by M. Froment-Meurice of Paris. *Industry of Nations*

Pearl scroll. *Spiers*

Bracelet of granite with silver linkings, by Rettie & Sons of Aberdeen. *Industry of Nations*

Lotus flowers filled with blue and red stones, by O. Weber. *The Workshop, Vol. 7*

Pearl-centered leaf.
Spiers

Turquoise centers and heart. *Spiers*

Designed by Prof. Ortwein of Germany.
The Workshop, Vol. 8

Handmade silver bracelet set with turquoise
and opal. *Sears Catalogue*

Sterling silver, hand-engraved
bangle. *Sears Catalogue*

Designed by Prof. R. Reinhardt of Stuttgart,
Germany. *The Workshop, Vol. 7*

Boars' tusk bracelet from
the Sandwich Islands. *Natural
History, America & Asia*

19th century Syrian silver bracelet. *Simple Jewelry.* □

Designed by M. Gueyton of Paris. *Industry of Nations*

Bracelets continued

Cast iron bracelet, by M. Devarannes of Berlin. *Industry of Nations*

Engraved scrolls.
Spiers

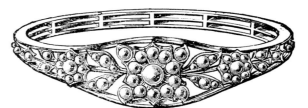

Oriental pearl bracelet. *Illustrated London News*

Cast iron bracelet, by M. Devarannes of Berlin. *Industry of Nations*

Gold bracelet set with rubies, by C. Rowlands & Son of London. *Industry of Nations*

Renaissance style bracelet from Stuttgart, Germany. *The Workshop, Vol. 5*

16th century French. *L'Art Pour Tous, Vol. 19*

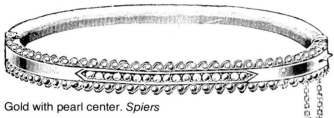

Gold with pearl center. *Spiers*

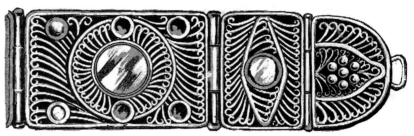

17th century Russian. *L'Art Pour Tous, Vol. 41*

Bangles from East India Museum,
London. *Century Dictionary, Vol. 1*

Pearls and turquoise. *Spiers*

Gold bracelet with embossed hearts.
Sears Catalogue

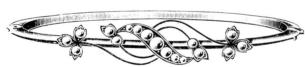

Gold link bracelet. *Spiers*

Diamond scrolls and pearls. *Spiers*

Gold bracelet. *Spiers*

Heavy embossed silver bracelet set with turquoise
and opal. *Sears Catalogue*

Bracelets continued

19th century English. *Spiers*

19th century gold engraved bracelet. *The Workshop, 1868*

African. *Natural History, Africa*

19th century English. *Spiers*

19th century English. *Spiers*

19th century English. *Spiers*

19th century English. *Spiers*

Bronze bracelet. *Iconographic*

19th century German. *The Workshop, 1871*

19th century German. *The Workshop, 1870*

19th century English. *Spiers*

19th century English. *Spiers*

19th century German. *The Workshop, 1871*

19th century English. *Spiers*

19th century English. *Spiers*

19th century English. *Spiers*

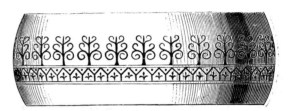

Silver bangle bracelet. *The Workshop, Vol. 2*

19th century English. *Spiers*

19th century German. *The Workshop, 1871*

19th century German. *The Workshop, 1866*

19th century English. *Spiers*

19th century English. *Spiers*

Brooches & Pins

The simplest form of brooch probably originated around 1000 B.C., during the Bronze Age, with the development of the safety pin, or fibula. This earliest form was little more than a stick pin bent in half, so that the point caught against the head of the pin. A slightly higher stage of development is evident in the fibulae found at Enkomi, in Cyprus, which date from the Mycenaean period. Very similar in appearance and in principle to the modern safety pin, the Mycenaean fibula had a coiled spring which forced the point against the catch.

From these relatively simple forms, the fibula developed in several different directions. Toward the end of the Bronze Age, fibulae became bow-shaped, an innovation which enabled them to gather more material together, and to hold it more securely. In the Iron Age, this bow was thickened and further modified, giving the fibula greater rigidity and leaving more surfaces for decoration.

The T-shaped, or "cross-bow" fibula, which developed during the geometric age of Greece, consisted of an exaggerated version of the vertical portion of the catchplate. During the first centuries of the Greek empire, this type of pin became extremely prevalent. Widely adopted and modified by other cultures, it was used in various forms for many centuries. Similar forms were even found in the tombs of Frankish and Teutonic warriors of the fifth to the ninth centuries A.D. More elaborately decorated than their predecessors, these fibulae had chased surfaces and were often surrounded by radial knobs.

Other types of brooches developed concurrently; some used thinly disguised versions of the safety pin attachment, while others depended on totally different methods. The medallion brooch, for example, was a stud used to fasten a cloak on the shoulders. Brilliantly decorated with inlaid stone, enamel, or paste, these circular brooches are well represented among Greek, Etruscan, and Roman jewelry deposits.

The animal brooch has also existed since ancient times. Animal forms were ubiquitous in every type of ancient jewelry. Decorations which assumed the shape of animals were first fixed as appendages to the fibulae; eventually they developed into the body of the brooch itself, with a pin similar to the modern brooch pin attached underneath.

In addition to the previously mentioned T-shaped fibulae, both the medallion and the animal brooch forms have been excavated from the tombs of Frankish and Teutonic warriors. Typically constructed of bronze, silver, or gold, they were often decorated with filigree work and inlaid with precious gems or enamel. The pins themselves, however, were nearly always made of iron.

In the Scandinavian countries, most of the early brooches were of the T-shaped variety, virtually indistinguishable from those of the same type found in the Frankish tombs. In time, these forms grew larger and more intricate. By the fifth and sixth centuries A.D., Scandinavian brooches had also incorporated animal forms into their designs.

During the Viking period in Scandinavia and nearby regions, (800-1050 A.D.), the brooch developed an oval, convex shape, somewhat resembling a tortoise. This shape appeared in the jewelry of northern Scotland, England, Ireland, Iceland, Normandy, and Livonia. Gradually, intricate, exquisitely decorated pieces evolved out of the basic tortoise shape. These lovely gold pieces, set with mosaics of turquoise, garnet, and mother-of-pearl in geometric patterns, abound in the Anglo-Saxon tombs of England.

In contrast to its counterparts, the Celtic brooch was largely penannular in shape, and sometimes quite big; examples have been found with pins measuring fifteen inches. Usually fashioned of bronze or silver, Celtic brooches were chased or engraved with intricate interlaced or dragonesque designs. Not surprisingly, they were similar in style to the illuminated Celtic manuscripts of the seventh, eighth, and ninth centuries.

Brooches of the Middle Ages were generally more simple than their predecessors. Characterized by a flat circular disk with an open center, they were often inscribed with religious, or sometimes "magical" formulas.

Extremely elaborate brooches were widely popular during the Renaissance. The trend culminated in the gaudy, oversized versions of the sixteenth and seventeenth centuries.

Light, floral patterns and pale, elegant colors

characterized European brooches of the eighteenth and nineteenth centuries. Gold work, which had lost its prestige and popularity with the ornate styles of the sixteenth and seventeenth centuries, regained its former prominence. Once again gold was used as a decoration in itself, rather than as background for collections of precious stones. The innovations of Rene Lalique in the late nineteenth and early twentieth centuries brought freshness and originality to old traditions in brooch design.

Although modern brooches incorporate various elements of all the styles described above, they tend to be more simple than ornate. Engraved gold work, inlaid with gems, enamel, or cameos, is characteristic of our age.

Designed by G. Mohring of Berlin. *Meyers*

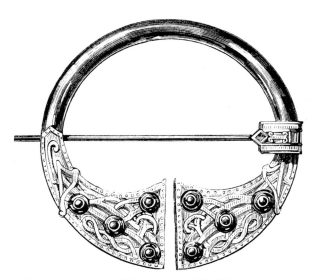

Bronze brooch, by Waterhouse of Dublin. *Industry of Nations*

Pearl balls with roll plate mounting. *Montgomery*

Silver brooch with pearls. *The Workshop, Vol. 1*

19th century French. *The Workshop, Vol. 5*

Brooches & Pins continued

19th century
German.
Meyers

19th century
English. *Spiers*

Diamond heart brooch. *Spiers*

Diamond brooch.
Spiers

19th century
English. *Spiers*

19th
century
German.
Meyers

Diamond and
enamel flower
brooch. *Spiers*

18th century Norwegian silver-gilt brooch. *Simple Jewelry* □

Gold stick pin with
one brilliant.
Montgomery

Gold pin with pearl
center. *Spiers*

Designed by H.
Hirzel of Berlin.
Meyers

Diamond and enamel
flower brooch. *Spiers*

Diamond
and enamel
horse
brooch.
Spiers

Diamond and
gold brooch.
Spiers

19th century French. *The Workshop, Vol. 5*

Bird of paradise in brilliants; 19th century French. *The Workshop, Vol. 8*

Gold pin. *Meyers*

Pearl and turquoise flower brooch. *Spiers*

19th century English pearl brooch. *Spiers*

Designed by H. van de Velde of Brussels. *Meyers*

Gold filigree with diamond center. *Spiers*

Brooch set with rubies and brilliants. *Meyers*

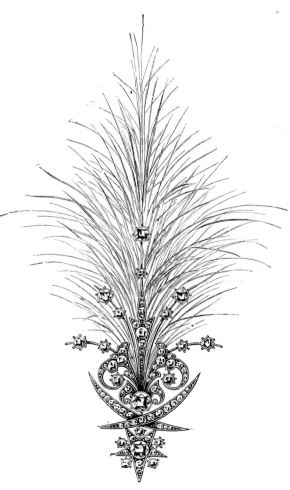

Diamond aigrette. *Spiers*

Brooches & Pins continued

Gold coil with brilliant. *Montgomery*

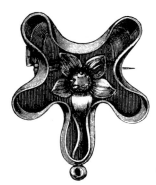

Designed by B. Mohring of Berlin. *Meyers*

19th century English gold brooch. *Spiers*

Pearl swallow brooch. *Spiers*

Pearl coronet brooch. *Spiers*

Pearl swallow brooch. *Spiers*

19th century English gold filigree brooch. *Spiers*

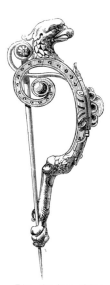

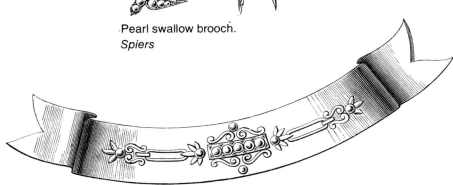

Brooch, designed by Blanvillain and Normand of Paris. *The Workshop, Vol. 7*

Pearl and turquoise brooch. *Spiers*

Pin, designed by A. Ortwein of Germany. *The Workshop, Vol. 8*

Diamond star brooch. *Spiers*

Gold brooch. *The Workshop, 1870*

19th century German. *Meyers*

Pearl brooch. *Spiers*

Pearl brooch. *Spiers*

Diamond and sapphire brooch. *Spiers*

Designed by M. Werner of Berlin. *Meyers*

Aiguillette (shoulder knot) with diamonds, pearls, and an emerald. *Industry of Nations*

Designed by H. Hirzel of Berlin. *Meyers*

19th century German. *The Workshop, 1868*

Engraved gold pin. *Montgomery*

Designed by von Rothmuller of Munich. *Meyers*

Roman gold wreath with enameled leaves and brilliants. *Montgomery*

Breast ornament, enameled and set with stones. *Industry of Nations*

Designed by M. Werner of Berlin. *Meyers*

19th century brooch. *The Workshop, Vol. 1*

Gold brooch with amethysts. *Montgomery*

Brooches & Pins continued

Turquoise and
pearl circle brooch.
Spiers

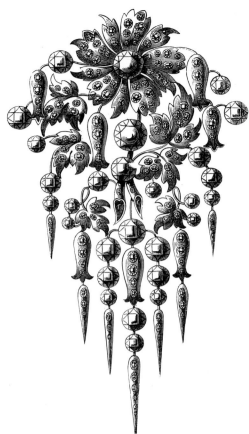

Gold brooch. *Meyers*

Polished sword with brilliants in handle.
Montgomery

Brooch set with diamonds and
pearls. *The Workshop, Vol. 5*

Gold filigree with pearl horseshoe
and diamond center. *Spiers*

Pearl spray brooch. *Spiers*

19th century German gold brooch.
The Workshop, 1869

19th century English pearl brooch.
Spiers

Silver brooch with gems. *The
Workshop, 1870*

Pearl horse head. *Montgomery*

Silver brooch with gems. *The Workshop, 1870*

Renaissance style brooch. *Meyers*

Designed by von Rothmuller of Munich. *Meyers*

Ruby and diamond trefoils. *Spiers*

Gold brooch. *The Workshop, Vol. 1*

Enameled handle with brilliant pendant. *Montgomery*

Diamond brooch. *Century Magazine, 1892*

Designed by C. Rowlands & Son of London. *Industry of Nations*

19th century English gold filigree brooch. *Spiers*

Pearl flower and spray brooch. *Spiers*

Pin, manufactured by M. Levy Prins of Brussels. *Industry of Nations*

Brooches & Pins continued

Gold brooch with brilliant center. *Montgomery*

Diamond brooch. *Century Magazine, 1892*

Pin, manufactured by M. Levy Prins of Brussels. *Industry of Nations*

Pearl crescent and swallow brooch. *Spiers*

Jewel inlaid brooch, designed by M. Froment-Meurice of Paris. *Industry of Nations*

Pearls and turquoise drops brooch. *Spiers*

Etruscan brooch. *L'Art Pour Tous, Vol. 16*

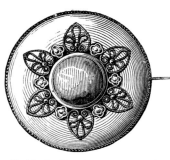

Gold pin. *The Workshop, 1871*

Jewel inlaid brooch, designed by M. Froment-Meurice of Paris. *Industry of Nations*

Brooch, designed by West of Dublin. *Industry of Nations*

Gold dagger stick pin with stones in handle. *Montgomery*

Pearl new moon and swallow. *Spiers*

Diamond brooch. *Century Magazine*

Pearl brooch. *Spiers*

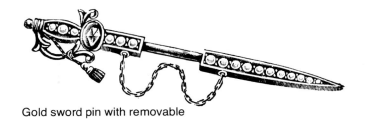

Gold sword pin with removable scabbard. *Montgomery*

Pearl brooch. *Spiers*

Gold brooch. *Meyers*

Designed by Mayer & Pleuer of Stuttgart, Germany. *The Workshop, Vol. 7*

Brooch, designed by Mayer & Pleuer of Stuttgart, Germany. *The Workshop, 1874*

Diamond brooch, designed by Phillips Bros. of London. *Industry of Nations*

Pearl hand with brilliant ring. *Montgomery*

Designed by B. Mohring of Berlin. *Meyers*

19th century German. *The Workshop, Vol. 5*

Brooches & Pins continued

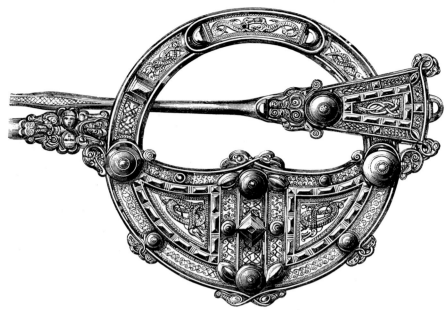

Bronze brooch with niello and gems, by Waterhouse of Dublin. *Industry of Nations*

Pin, manufactured by M. Levy Prins of Brussels. *Industry of Nations*

19th century English diamond brooch. *Spiers*

19th century French. *The Workshop, Vol. 8*

Pearl and diamond brooch. *Montgomery*

19th century German. *The Workshop, Vol. 1*

Diamond scroll brooch. *Spiers*

Gold brooch. *The Workshop, 1868*

Designed by F. Friedlander of Berlin. *Meyers*

Diamond and ruby brooch. *Spiers*

Breast ornament, enameled and set with stones. *Industry of Nations*

Designed by M.A. Nicolai of Munich. *Meyers*

Brooch, designed by West of Dublin. *Industry of Nations*

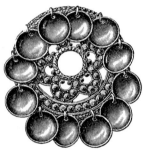

Norwegian brooch. *Meyers*

Coil scarf pin with diamond center. *Montgomery*

19th century gold brooch. *The Workshop, Vol. 7*

Gold brooch. *The Workshop, Vol. 1*

Diamond brooch, designed by C. Rowlands & Son of London. *Industry of Nations*

Pin, manufactured by M. Levy Prins of Brussels. *Industry of Nations*

Brooches & Pins continued

19th century French. *The Workshop, Vol. 8*

French silver brooch set with pearls and diamonds. *The Workshop, 1871*

Gold brooch. *Meyers*

Diamond and gold brooch. *Spiers*

Brooch, designed by West of Dublin. *Industry of Nations*

19th century brooch. *The Workshop, Vol. 1*

Gold brooch with rubies. *Montgomery*

Gold brooch with diamond center. *Montgomery*

17th century Russian brooch. *L'art Pour Tous, Vol. 41*

Pearl swallow brooch. *Spiers*

Gold brooch with pearls. *The Workshop, 1868*

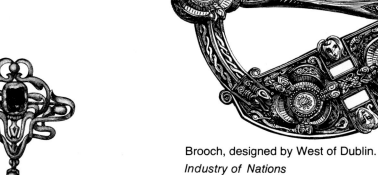

Brooch, designed by West of Dublin. *Industry of Nations*

Designed by O. Gack of Munich. *Meyers*

Gold brooch. *Montgomery*

Gold brooch with ruby center. *Montgomery*

Brooches & Pins continued

Bronze brooch with gems, by Waterhouse of Dublin. *Industry of Nations*

Gold and jewelled brooch, designed by Ellis & Son of Exeter, England. *Industry of Nations*

Designed by Mayer & Pleuer of Stuttgart, Germany. *The Workshop, Vol. 7*

19th century French pin. *The Workshop, Vol. 5*

Pearl brooch. *Spiers*

Pearl brooch. *Spiers*

French fibula. *Meyers*

Silver brooch set with brilliants. *The Workshop, 1871*

Brooch, manufactured by Watherston & Brogden of London. *Industry of Nations*

Indian brooch constructed of brass. *Industry of Nations*

Silver brooch, designed by Ellis & Son of Exeter, England. *Industry of Nations*

Renaissance style brooch. *The Workshop, 1873*

Turquoise and pearl flower brooch. *Spiers*

Diamond brooch set in green and gold enamel. *Industry of Nations*

Gold and pearl safety pin. *Spiers*

Designed by Mayer & Pleuer of Stuttgart, Germany. *The Workshop, Vol. 7*

Irish heavy-headed pin of inlaid bronze, for both men and women. *Century Magazine, Vol. 38*

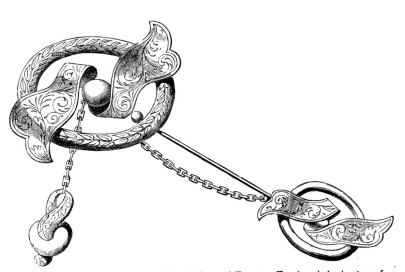

Silver brooch, designed by Ellis & Son of Exeter, England. *Industry of Nations*

Brooches & Pins continued

Breast ornament, enameled and set with stones. *Industry of Nations*

Designed by B. Mohring of Berlin. *Meyers*

Bronze brooch, by Waterhouse of Dublin. *Industry of Nations*

19th century German. *The Workshop, Vol. 5*

19th century French brooch. *The Workshop, Vol. 5*

Humming-bird in brilliants, sapphires, emerald, and rubies. *Industry of Nations*

Designed by H. Hirzel of Berlin. *Meyers*

Diamond and sapphire bow with pearl drops. *Spiers*

Pearl swallow brooch. *Spiers*

Rope twist scarf pin with diamond center. *Montgomery*

Colored gold leaf brooch with three diamonds. *Montgomery*

Breast ornament, enameled and set with stones. *Industry of Nations*

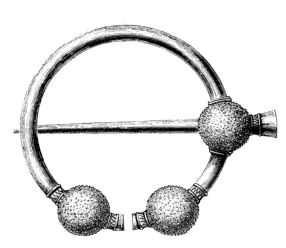

Bronze brooch, by Waterhouse of Dublin. *Industry of Nations*

Brooch, designed by S. H. & D. Gass of London. *Industry of Nations*

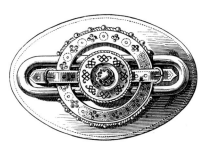

Brooch, designed by G. Ehni of Stuttgart, Germany. *The Workshop, Vol. 1*

Roman coil brooch with diamond center. *Montgomery*

19th century brooch with pearls and diamonds. *Industry of Nations*

Gold brooch with carbuncle and brilliants, designed by C. Rowlands & Son of London. *Industry of Nations*

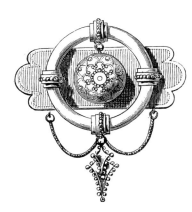

Brooch, designed by G. Ehni of Stuttgart, Germany. *The Workshop, Vol. 1*

Brooches & Pins continued

Gold brooch with gems. *The Workshop, 1868*

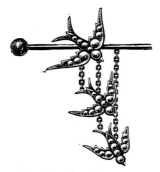

Pin, manufactured by M. Levy Prins of Brussels. *Industry of Nations*

Pearl swallow brooch. *Spiers*

Pin, designed by A. Ortwein of Germany. *The Workshop, Vol. 8*

Pearl and diamond brooch. *Montgomery*

Designed by M. Werner of Berlin. *Meyers*

19th century French brooch. *The Workshop, Vol. 5*

Silver leaf stick pin. *Montgomery*

Gold brooch. *The Workshop, Vol. 1*

Designed by G. Morren of Antwerp. *Meyers*

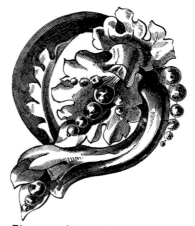

Pin, manufactured by M. Levy Prins of Brussels. *Industry of Nations*

Designed by M.A. Nicolai of Munich. *Meyers*

19th century German. *The Workshop, Vol. 1*

Brooch, designed by G. Ehni of Stuttgart, Germany. *The Workshop, Vol. 1*

Fibula. *Meyers*

Fibula. *Meyers*

19th century French brooch. *The Workshop, Vol. 5*

Steel brooch, designed by W. Harry Rogers of London. *Industry of Nations*

Gold stick pin with one brilliant. *Montgomery*

Brooch, designed and manufactured by H. Schefer of Berlin. *The Workshop, Vol. 5*

13th century French gold brooch, set with rubies and sapphires. *Simple Jewelry* □

Tara brooch of gold and white bronze; back view. *Industry of Nations*

Brooches & Pins continued

Brooch, with diamonds and pearls. *Spiers*

Designed by von Rothmuller of Munich. *Meyers*

Designed by Vernier of Paris. *Meyers*

19th century German gold brooch. *The Workshop, 1869*

Butterfly pin. *The Workshop, 1871*

Pearl tie brooch. *Spiers*

Designed by A. Charpentier of Paris. *Meyers*

Roman enameled battle ax. *Montgomery*

Etruscan brooch. *L'Art Pour Tous, Vol. 16*

Gold stick pin with three brilliants. *Montgomery*

Gold stick pin with brilliants. *Montgomery*

Pearl spray safety pin. *Spiers*

Gold dagger stick pin with stones in handle. *Montgomery*

Pearl and turquoise circle brooch. *Spiers*

19th century German. *Meyers*

Etruscan brooch. *L'Art Pour Tous, Vol. 16*

Designed by O. Roty of Paris. *Meyers*

Silver leaf with gilt center. *Montgomery*

Pin, designed and manufactured by H. Schaper of Berlin. *The Workshop, Vol. 7*

Horseshoe and whip with brilliants. *Montgomery*

Brooch, manufactured by M. Rudolph of Paris. *Industry of Nations*

Designed by B. Mohring of Berlin. *Meyers*

Gold cornet stick pin. *Montgomery*

Designed by J. Dampt of Paris. *Meyers*

Designed by G. Morren of Antwerp. *Meyers*

Designed by Chaplain of Paris. *Meyers*

Gold scimitar. *Montgomery*

Gold stick pin with diamond and pearl. *Montgomery*

Gold pin. *The Workshop, 1871*

Diamond brooch. *Century Magazine, 1892*

Pearl safety pin. *Spiers*

Gold brooch with amethyst center. *Montgomery*

Roman gold leaves with two pearls. *Montgomery*

Designed by J. Cheret of Paris. *Meyers*

Cameos

The cameo is a small carving in relief, usually fashioned on striated precious or semi-precious stones, and occasionally on shell. Originating in the East as a decoration on the reverse of seals, the cameo was developed in Greece in the fourth century B.C.

The import of certain minerals which were ideal for making cameos, such as the chalcedonic variety of quartz, onyx, and sardonyx, from India and other Eastern nations, stimulated the development of this art in the West. Sardonyx, a favorite material of the ancient cameo cutters, was ideal because of its natural layers of color—sometimes white and black, sometimes white, black, and brown. The design was cut into the lighter-colored vein of the stone, with the dark-colored vein serving as the background.

Because of the increased trade between Greece and the Orient following the death of Alexander the Great, larger quantities of the materials necessary for making cameos became available in the West. This fact naturally led to an abundance of cameo designs; indeed, cameos not only decorated jewelry, but were also cut into jeweled caskets, vases, cups, and candelabra.

Cameo designs usually depict portrait heads or busts. In the Roman era, however, more ambitious designs were executed, for during that time, the art reached a zenith of excellence and intricacy which has never been surpassed. One famous example of the Romans' expertise is the Great Agate of the Sainte Chapelle, now in the Bibliotheque Nationale in Paris. It is a sardonyx consisting of five irregular shaped layers measuring twelve inches by ten and a half inches. Representations of all the deified members of the house of Julian appear on the upper third of the piece. In the center is a depiction of the reception by the Emperor Tiberius and his wife Livia of Germanicus, who has returned from a successful German campaign. The lower third is filled with the dejected and woeful faces of a group of Germanicus's captives.

After a long period during which the popularity of cameos declined, the art form was resurrected during the Renaissance. As is the case with all types of jewelry, the popularity of cameos has increased and waned according to the dictates of fashion. For long periods of time, no cameos would be worn; then suddenly they would burst upon the fashion scene once again. Cameos were particularly in vogue during the Victorian era; those which have survived to this day attest to their elegant beauty.

Today, despite the relatively low value of its materials, the cameo is highly regarded artistically and financially. Antique pieces are particularly prized by collectors.

16th century French; profile of unknown empress. *L'Art Pour Tous, Vol. 8*

White and brown shell cameo; portrait head in high relief. *Connoisseur, Vol. 2* □

16th century French; profile of Julius Caesar. *L'Art Pour Tous, Vol. 8*

16th century French. *L'Art Pour Tous, Vol. 7*

Renaissance style work, designed by J. J. Schnorr of Stuttgart, Germany. *The Workshop, Vol. 5*

Designed by M. Julie of Liège, France. *Industry of Nations*

16th century French. *L'Art Pour Tous, Vol. 8*

Cameo necklace, designed by G. Ehni of Stuttgart, Germany. *The Workshop, Vol. II*

Cameos continued

Designed by Mayer & Pleuer of Stuttgart, Germany. *The Workshop, 1870*

Designed by M. Julin of Liège, France. *Industry of Nations*

19th century German. *The Workshop, 1872*

16th century French. *L'Art Pour Tous, Vol. 7*

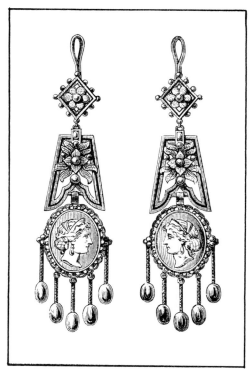

Earrings with mounted cameos. *The Workshop, Vol. 1*

Renaissance style work, designed by J. Schnorr of Stuttgart, Germany. *The Workshop, Vol. 5*

16th century French. *L'Art Pour Tous, Vol. 8*

16th century French. *L'Art Pour Tous, Vol. 7*

16th century French. *L'Art Pour Tous, Vol. 7*

16th century French. *L'Art Pour Tous, Vol. 8*

Cameo earring, designed by G. Ehni of Stuttgart, Germany. *The Workshop, 1871*

19th century German. *The Workshop, 1870*

16th century French. *L'Art Pour Tous, Vol. 7*

19th century German. *The Workshop, 1868*

17th century German cameo in amethyst and carnelion. *Connoisseur, Vol. 5* □

17th century Russian. *L'Art Pour Tous, Vol. 41*

Cameos continued

Designed by M. Julin of Liège, France. *Industry of Nations*

Renaissance style work, designed by J. Schnorr of Stuttgart, Germany. *The Workshop, Vol. 5*

Designed by Mayer & Pleuer of Stuttgart, Germany. *The Workshop, 1870*

Designed by G. Ehni of Stuttgart, Germany. *L'Art Pour Tous, 1871*

19th century French. *The Workshop, Vol. 5*

Designed by Mayer & Pleuer of Stuttgart, Germany. *The Workshop, Vol. 5*

Brooch; cameo
surrounded by
diamonds on blue
enamel, designed by
Phillips Bros. of
London. *Industry of
Nations*

16th century French; profile of
unknown empress. *L'Art Pour
Tous, Vol. 8*

16th century French. *L'Art Pour
Tous, Vol. 7*

19th century bracelet with mounted cameo. *The Workshop, Vol. 1*

Designed by H. Schefer of Berlin.
The Workshop, Vol. 5

16th century French; profile of
Julius Caesar. *L'Art Pour
Tous, Vol. 8*

Mounted cameo brooch.
The Workshop, Vol. 1

16th century French. *L'Art
Pour Tous, Vol. 8*

Renaissance
style German.
*The Workshop,
1869*

Chains

A chain consists of a series of links, usually made of metal, connected together in such a way that the whole forms a flexible band or cord. Chains have been used throughout history as symbols of office or state, as insignia of orders of knighthood, and as personal decorations. Chains have been worn around necks, wrists, and ankles, alone or hung with pearls, gems, watches, or other pendants; the versatility of the chain knows no bounds.

The chain is probably one of the most familiar as well as one of the most useful of devices. Its origin is ancient; indeed, remnants of Roman chains can be found in collections of most of the world's renowned museums.

In the Middle Ages, particularly during the reign of Richard II (1377-1399), a revival of the art of chain-making brought a new popularity to their use. Heavy, twisted links of gold and silver were worn by both men and women of the upper classes during this period, although during the reign of Charles I (1625-1649), chains were largely neglected as personal decorations for men.

Chains are divided into two general classifications, based on the fundamental forms of their links. Coil chains consist of a series of links which are usually oval in shape; these interlock by passing through one another. Block chains are constructed of flat bars which are joined together by cylindrical pins so that the bars do not interconnect.

Within these two general classifications are many smaller, more specific types of chains, such as the link chain, pitch chain, and sprocket chain of the block type; and the open link chain, studded link chain, twisted link chain, safety chain, ladder chain, and jack chain—all under the general classification of coil chains. Many of these have decorative value as well as the strength and durability necessary for mechanical and industrial purposes.

Ornamental chains are most often constructed of brass, bronze, gold, or silver. Before the dawn of the age of mechanization, chains were, of course, made solely by hand; now, they are almost exclusively manufactured by machine. In either case, the process is the same: the chain is made by forging each link separately, then welding them together to form a single strand.

19th century man's
two-strand rolled gold chain.
Sears Catalogue

19th century English; gold chain with turquoise. *Spiers*

Men's engraved gold vest chain. *Montgomery*

19th century English; dog link. *Spiers*

Gold curb chain. *Spiers*

19th century English gold chain. *Spiers*

19th century English gold chain. *Spiers*

Ladies' Victoria chain with enameled charm. *Montgomery*

19th century gold traced link chain. *Sears Catalogue*

Men's silver vest chain. *Montgomery*

Chains continued

19th century English; gold chain with opal and crystal. *Spiers*

19th century English gold chain. *Spiers*

19th century English gold chain. *Spiers*

19th century English gold chain. *Spiers*

19th century English gold chain. *Spiers*

Men's engraved gold vest chain. *Montgomery*

Men's gold vest chain. *Montgomery*

19th century gold chain, set with almandine stones. *Sears Catalogue*

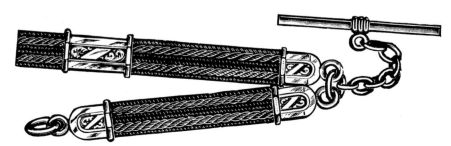

Men's silver vest chain. *Montgomery*

Ladies' roll plate extension vest chain. *Montgomery*

19th century English; fetter and knot. *Spiers*

19th century English. *Handbook of Ornament*

19th century gold soldered rope chain. *Sears Catalogue*

Men's gold vest chain. *Montgomery*

19th century English; fetter and one link. *Spiers*

19th century English; close graduated curb. *Spiers*

Ladies' Victoria chain and charm, with six brilliants in center. *Montgomery*

Ladies' Victoria chain with pink pearl opera glasses. *Montgomery*

19th century English; gold chain with turquoise. *Spiers*

19th century man's two-strand gold rope chain. *Sears Catalogue*

Chains continued

19th century three-strand rolled gold chain. *Sears Catalogue*

Ladies' Victoria chain with pearl horn charm. *Montgomery*

Ladies' two-strand Victoria chain with turquoise set in heart. *Montgomery*

19th century English gold chain. *Spiers*

19th century man's gold engraved chain. *Sears Catalogue*

19th century English gold chain. *Spiers*

19th century English gold chain. *Spiers*

19th century English gold chain. *Spiers*

19th century English gold chain. *Spiers*

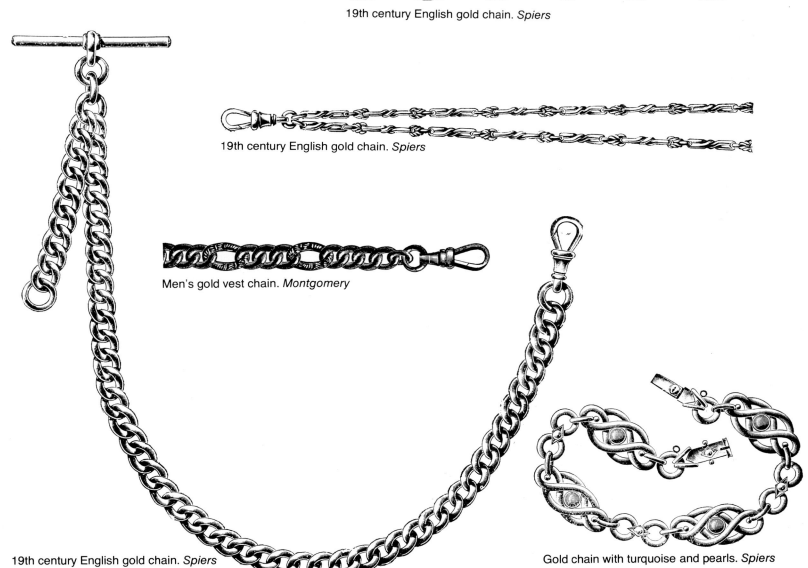

Men's gold vest chain. *Montgomery*

19th century English gold chain. *Spiers*

Gold chain with turquoise and pearls. *Spiers*

Crosses

The cross has been used as both a religious symbol and as an ornament since long before the Christian era. The artifacts of India, Syria, Persia, and Egypt, for example, have all yielded beautiful examples of ornamental crosses. As a religious symbol, the cross has been almost universal; in most cases, its early use was connected with some form of nature worship.

There are many shapes and classifications of crosses. The most common is the Latin cross, in which the upright stem is longer than the transom. With two transoms, the cross is called an archiepiscopal or patriarchal cross; with three transoms, a papal cross. A cross with two transoms and a slanting crosspiece below is commonly used by Slavs and other Eastern peoples. The Greek design has two limbs of equal length. St. Andrew's cross is shaped like an "X," and the Tau cross resembles a "T." The Celtic cross, also known as the Iona cross, has a circle in the center. The Maltese cross and the swastika are still more elaborate examples of crosses.

The death of Jesus Christ on the cross conferred a new significance to the emblem. The cross was almost immediately adopted as a symbol of Christianity, although its use was restricted and secret until the time of Constantine. The iconoclasts of the Byzantine era attacked the practice of using the cross as a religious symbol, but the Second Council of Nicaea vindicated the practice in 787.

The crucifix, a cross with the figure of Jesus depicted upon it, became popular quite early in Christian history. At first, the figures were painted or portrayed in bas-relief, and the scenes were mainly representations of the Saviour reigning, in robe and crown. In the Christian East, this style of crucifix has survived to the modern age, however, in the West, the figure of Jesus dying on the cross has predominated. This particular portrayal has become a universal symbol for Roman Catholicism. For the most part, modern Protestants have abandoned the use of the crucifix in preference for the Latin cross.

In the Middle Ages, in addition to being a religious ornament, the cross predominated in architecture and design as a symbol of honor. It appeared abundantly, for example, on flags, coats of arms, and orders of knighthood. As personal ornamentation, the cross was often hung from a chain around the neck; because it hangs over the chest, this type of cross is called a pectoral cross.

The Middle Ages and the Renaissance produced beautiful examples of crosses, often fashioned of gold and enamel, with intricately worked designs or scenes portrayed on one or both sides.

French cross set with brilliants. *The Workshop, 1871*

19th century German, designed by
G. Ehni of Stuttgart, Germany. *The
Workshop, Vol. 6*

Designed by G. Ehni of Stuttgart
Germany. *The Workshop, Vol. 6*

Byzantine cross of gilt copper. *Masterpieces of Industrial Art*

Renaissance style necklace with dangling cross, designed by A. Ortwein of Germany. *The Workshop, Vol. 8*

Crosses continued

German. *Meyers*

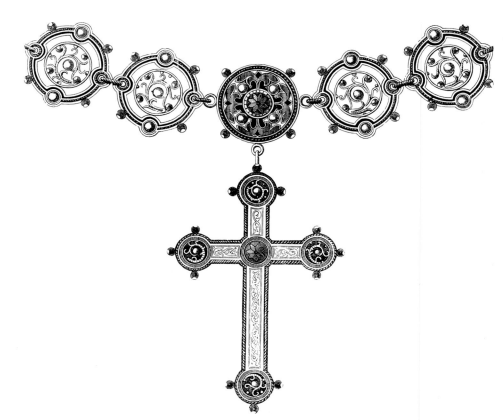

19th century German necklace with dangling cross. *The Workshop, 1871*

Renaissance style German. *The Workshop, 1869*

19th century French, designed by A. Leroy of Paris. *The Workshop, Vol. 7*

Spanish. *L'Art Pour Tous, Vol. 28*

Designed by G. Ehni of Stuttgart, Germany. *The Workshop, Vol. 6*

Spanish. *L'Art Pour Tous, Vol. 28*

Modern Austrian rosary of ebony and ivory beads, with cross of silver. *Simple Jewelry* □

19th century German; gold. *The Workshop, 1873*

19th century German, designed by G. Ehni of Stuttgart, Germany. *The Workshop, Vol. 6*

Crowns & Tiaras

The crown probably evolved from the Eastern diadem—a richly embroidered band of linen, silk, or flexible gold which was worn tied around the head. More elaborate than its predecessor, the crown is constructed from a band of metal, such as iron, bronze, gold, or silver, and it has an upper row of ornament, usually consisting of gems set into the metal.

The term "tiara" designates a bee-hive shaped, triple-crowned headpiece. The papal tiara (which in its present form dates from the Renaissance) employs a triple crown to symbolize the pope's authority over heaven, earth, and hell.

Ornamental headbands, such as diadems, crowns, and tiaras, originally had no regal significance. The original decorative headband, a garland or wreath made up of leaves or flowers, was conferred upon the winners of athletic games during the Hellenistic era.

The Romans adopted this practice, using the wreath to confer honor for other distinctions and for services rendered. The returning conqueror's crown of laurels, the crown of myrtle, the bridal and the funeral crowns were all devised by the Romans. Some ancient Roman coins have been discovered which depict emporers wearing stellate or spike crowns on their heads, but these crowns were probably ornamental, with no imperial significance.

Among the most famous crowns in Europe is the Iron Crown of Lombardy, which is included among this collection of pictures. Richly jeweled and enameled, it consists of an iron band enclosed in a circlet made up of six hinged plates of gold. This crown is greatly revered, for it is believed that the inner band of iron was hammered out of one of the original nails of the cross upon which Christ was crucified. Its minature size (only six inches in diameter) has caused doubt among experts that it was ever really intended to be worn.

Imperial crowns probably originated more than a thousand years ago, with the first English coronation ritual. The coronation ritual, with the requisite crown, was eventually adopted by many European countries. The earliest English crowns were helmet-shaped. By the fifteenth century, one or more arches were incorporated onto the rim, and they sometimes crossed at the raised center. This center was often formed by a ball and cross, later replaced in most of Europe by a fleur-de-lis. Another form of crown used in England and other parts of Europe was a wreath-like band of gold, encrusted with a string of jewels and tied at the back.

Many of the European royal crowns were made of sections which were connected by hinges and long pins. These hinges enabled the crown to be taken apart easily for transport or storage. And since the crown would be worn by numerous royal personages, the hinges made it adjustable for proper fit.

Although many European countries still possess royal crowns among their jewel collections, only two European states—England and the Vatican—still employ these ornaments in the course of state ceremonies.

Persian crown. *Illustrated London News*

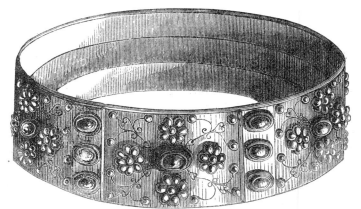

Iron crown of Lombardy. *Harper's, Vol. 43*

Diadem in silver and silver-gilt with pearls and emeralds. *The Workshop, Vol. 8*

Imperial crown. *Illustrated London News*

Coronation crown of H. M. the Queen, Tower of London. *Illustrated London News*

The crown of Charlemagne. *Terms in Art*

Crowns & Tiaras continued

Silver diadem with brilliants and white Oriental pearls, designed by Ritter Theophil von Hansen, manufactured by A.E. Kochert of Vienna.
The Workshop, Vol. 7

Diadem, designed by A. Leroy of Paris. *The Workshop, Vol. 7*

Gold diadem with sapphires and emeralds, designed and manufactured by A.E. Kochert of Vienna. *The Workshop, Vol. 7*

Sapphire and diamond tiara, by M. Lemonier of Paris. *Industry of Nations*

Coronation crown of H.M. the Queen, Tower of London. *Illustrated London News*

Earrings

The earliest mention of earrings in recorded history occurs in the Book of Genesis, where they are referred to as talismans belonging to the family of Jacob. It was quite common among ancient peoples to use earrings as amulets or talismans; thus, for example, aboriginal tribes in New Zealand often decorated their earrings with sharks' teeth or with the teeth of enemies, in order to ward off evil.

From the earliest time, earrings were worn suspended from the ear by means of a ring or hook passing through the pendulous lobe of the ear. Among primitive tribes, earrings were remarkable for their enormous size. In Borneo, the Berawan people use plugs three and three-quarter inches in diameter through the lobe of the ear. A Masai earplug has been found which was made of stone, weighing nearly three pounds and measuring four and a half inches in diameter. According to the Masai standards of fashion, the earlobes were supposed to be enlarged so that they could be stretched long enough to meet each other at the top of the head.

Among most peoples, today and at earlier stages of history, style dictates that two earrings be worn, one suspended from each earlobe, and that the two earrings resemble each other as closely as possible. Some Oriental peoples, however, have preferred adorning only one ear. This style has been adopted by some young people in Western Europe and the United States. In recent years, some young people have gone to the other extreme by wearing two or more earrings in the same ear.

Different cultures also varied in their approach to the question of which sex should wear earrings. In most Oriental countries, both sexes commonly wore earrings. In Babylonia, and later in Assyria, men wore earrings to denote their rank and status. Earrings for males, however, were the exception rather than the rule. The Hebrews and Egyptians, as well as the Greeks and Romans, allowed only their women to wear earrings, and this style is followed in most of Europe and America today.

We have many examples of ancient earrings from the tombs and statues of Egypt, Assyria, Troy, the Mycenaean period at Enkomi, and Cyprus, particularly from the tombs of the Greek settlers who lived in the fourth century B.C. The earliest Egyptian earrings were huge gold loops, but gradually they became smaller and were hung with long pendants. Cyprian earrings used animal figures, particularly bulls, as decorations. Though Roman earrings were more simply designed, they were the first to be adorned with precious stones and pearls. The Romans also had the distinction of being the first—and possibly the only—culture to attach earrings to the ears of their pets. Antonia, the daughter of Marc Antony and the wife of Drusus (38–9 B.C.) is said to have attached a pair of earrings to her pet lamprey.

The extravagant headdresses which were in vogue during the Middle Ages rendered earrings impractical. The Renaissance, however, saw a vigorous revival of this form of personal decoration; indeed, even men of this era began to wear earrings. Pearls, which enjoyed a growing popularity especially in Europe, were commonly used to decorate earrings in the eighteenth century; the nineteenth century saw the revival of the cameo.

Earrings have enjoyed an undiminished popularity in modern times, consisting today of many different reproductions and adaptations of historical models. At the beginning of this century, a screw device (called a post) for attaching the earring to the ear was invented. This has led to a variety of new, original styles, which are generally less extravagant than the Renaissance styles but quite beautiful in their own right.

Roman gold ear-drop with diamond center. *Montgomery*

Designed by G. Ehni of Stuttgart, Germany. *The Workshop, Vol. 1*

Designed by H. Schefer of Berlin. *The Workshop, Vol. 7*

Roman gold ear-drop with turquoise center. *Montgomery*

Gold Roman earring. *L'Art Pour Tous, Vol. 8*

19th century German. *The Workshop, 1866*

German Renaissance style. *The Workshop, Vol. 8*

French earring. *The Workshop, Vol. 5*

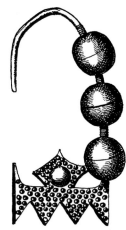

18th century Russian. *L'Art Pour Tous, Vol. 41*

Designed by G. Ehni of Stuttgart, Germany. *The Workshop, Vol. 1*

18th century Russian. *L'Art Pour Tous, Vol. 41*

Etruscan earring, in the Louvre Museum. *L'Art Pour Tous, Vol. 31*

Designed by A. Pleuer of Stuttgart, Germany. *The Workshop, Vol. 7*

19th century German. *The Workshop, Vol. 5*

19th century German. *The Workshop, 1866*

Earring set with brilliants. *The Workshop, Vol. 8*

Earrings continued

Gold
heart-shaped
earring. *The
Workshop, 1870*

Gold Roman
earring. *L'Art Pour
Tous, Vol. 8*

7th century Byzantine gold earrings. *Simple Jewelry* □

19th century
German. *The
Workshop, 1872*

Gold
heart-shaped
earring. *The
Workshop, 1870*

Designed by G.
Ehni of Stuttgart,
Germany. *The
Workshop, Vol. 6*

Renaissance
style. *The
Workshop, 1873*

Designed by A.
Pleuer of
Stuttgart,
Germany. *The
Workshop, Vol. 7*

Cameo earring.
*The Workshop,
Vol. 1*

Renaissance style. *The Workshop, 1873*

19th century German. *The Workshop, 1869*

Designed by B. Franffe in Paris. *The Workshop, 1872*

Designed by G. Ehni of Stuttgart, Germany. *The Workshop, Vol.6*

Gold Roman earring. *L'Art Pour Tous, Vol. 8*

Designed by G. Ehni of Stuttgart, Germany. *The Workshop, 1873*

19th century German. *The Workshop, Vol. 1*

19th century French. *The Workshop, Vol. 1*

Renaissance style. *The Workshop, 1868*

19th century German. *The Workshop, Vol. 7*

Earrings continued

Designed by A. Leroy of Paris. *The Workshop, Vol. 7*

Panther's head earring; Roman. *L'Art Pour Tous, Vol. 8*

19th century German. *The Workshop, 1866*

19th century German. *The Workshop, 1871*

19th century German, from Stuttgart. *The Workshop, 1870*

19th century German, from Stuttgart. *The Workshop, 1870*

19th century German. *The Workshop, Vol. 5*

Gold Roman earring with dove ornament. *L'Art Pour Tous, Vol. 8*

Etruscan earring, in the Louvre Museum. *L'Art Pour Tous, Vol. 31*

Flower basket earring, made of gold. *L'Art Pour Tous, Vol. 8*

Silver earring set with diamonds and pearls. *The Workshop, Vol. 7*

19th century French. *The Workshop, Vol. 7*

19th century German, from Stuttgart. *The Workshop, 1870*

Etruscan. *L'Art Pour Tous, Vol. 16*

Designed by A. Leroy of Paris. *The Workshop, Vol. 7*

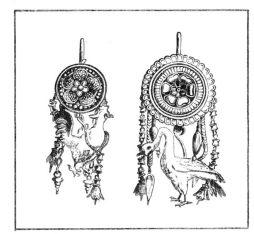

Etruscan earring of gold enamel. *Masterpieces of Industrial Art*

19th century French. *The Workshop, 1872*

Designed by A. Pleuer of Stuttgart, Germany. *The Workshop, Vol. 7*

Greek gold earring. *Masterpieces of Industrial Art*

18th century Russian. *L'Art Pour Tous, Vol. 41*

Etruscan earring, in the Louvre Museum. *L'Art Pour Tous, Vol. 31*

19th century German. *The Workshop, 1866*

18th century Russian. *L'Art Pour Tous, Vol.41*

Designed by Meyer & Pleuer of Stuttgart, Germany. *The Workshop, Vol. 5*

Earrings continued

19th century
French. *The
Workshop, Vol. 5*

Designed by Hugo
Schaper in Berlin. *The
Workshop, 1871*

19th century
German. *The
Workshop, 1866*

19th century
German. *The
Workshop, 1872*

Designed by H.
Schefer of Berlin.
*The Workshop,
Vol. 7*

Diamond earrings,
designed by M.
Baugrand of Paris.
The Workshop, Vol. 7

18th century Russian. *L'Art Pour
Tous, Vol. 41*

19th century
German, from
Stuttgart. *The
Workshop, 1870*

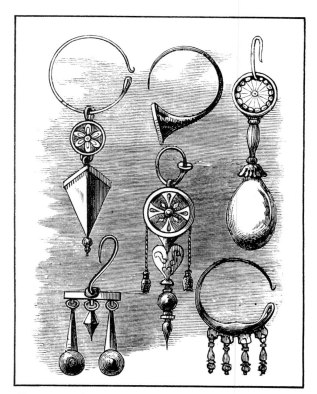

Roman earrings. *Harper's, Vol. 46*

19th century
German. *The
Workshop, 1869*

Gold Roman
earring. *The
Workshop, 1869*

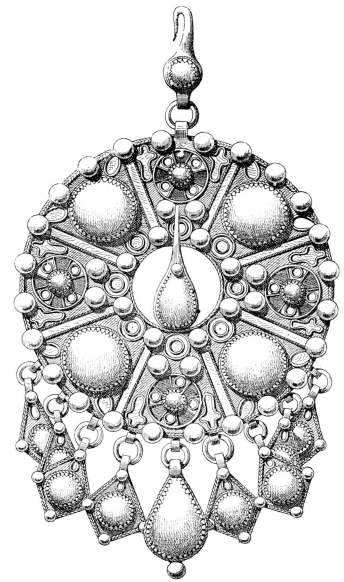

19th century Arabic. *L'Art Pour Tous, Vol. 14*

Designed by
Meyer & Pleuer of
Stuttgart,
Germany. *The
Workshop, Vol. 5*

Etruscan. *L'Art
Pour Tous, Vol. 16*

17th century Russian. *L'Art Pour
Tous, Vol. 41*

Diamond
earrings,
designed by M.
Baugrand of
Paris. *The
Workshop, Vol. 7*

Earring set with
brilliants. *The
Workshop, Vol. 8*

Earrings continued

19th century
German; gold.
The Workshop,
1869

19th century
French. *The*
Workshop, Vol. 5

19th century
German; gold.
The Workshop,
1869

19th century
German, from
Stuttgart. *The*
Workshop, Vol. 1

Gold Roman
earring. *The*
Workshop, 1869

Gold Roman
earring. *L'Art Pour*
Tous, Vol. 8

19th century
German. *The*
Workshop, Vol. 5

Gold earring,
designed by von
Demfelben. *The*
Workshop, 1870

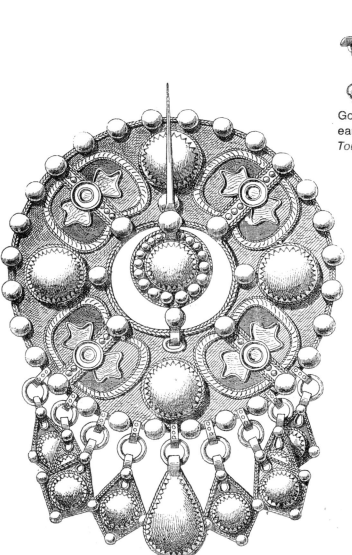

19th century Arabic. *L'Art Pour Tous, Vol. 14*

19th century
German. *The*
Workshop, 1866

19th century
French. *The*
Workshop, 1872

Earring found in the island of Rhodes; in the Louvre Museum. *Masterpieces of Industrial Art*

18th century Russian. *L'Art Pour Tous, Vol. 41*

Silver earring set with diamonds and pearls. *L'Art Pour Tous, Vol. 5*

19th century German. *The Workshop, 1871*

Designed by G. Ehni, of Stuttgart, Germany. *The Workshop, Vol. 1*

Gold satyr's head earring. *L'Art Pour Tous, Vol. 8*

Gold earring, designed by von Demfelben. *The Workshop, 1870*

Designed by A. Pleuer of Stuttgart, Gemany. *The Workshop, Vol. 7*

19th century French. *The Workshop, Vol. 7*

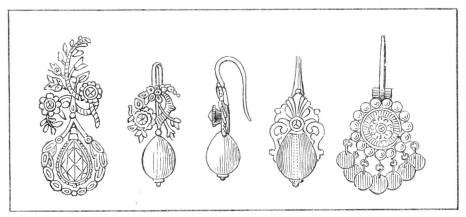

Earrings of the Middle East. *Land and Book*

Hair Ornaments & Combs

Jeweled ornaments for the hair and head, such as combs or aigrettes—sprays of gems—have been discovered dating back to ancient Egypt, Greece, and Rome. Some examples constructed of wood, bone, and horn have been found in Swiss lake dwellings. Egyptian hair ornaments were made of ivory; Greek and Roman specimens were usually fashioned of boxwood, although ebony, ivory, and metals were also used. Interestingly, Greek combs had teeth on both sides.

During the Middle Ages, the use of hair ornaments declined substantially. With the Renaissance, however, interest in this form of adornment was rekindled. Combs were not only used as decoration, but also as practical instruments for arranging the hair. Ornamental combs of the Renaissance were delicately carved by hand and inlaid with precious stones; their designs often copied ancient Greek and Roman relics. Tortoise-shell as material for making combs was popular during this period.

The use of the periwig by men, which originated in the mid-seventeenth century, produced a change in style whereby combs became fashionable for men as well women. Women's hair ornaments had by this time diversified, and now included various forms of the aigrette. During the eighteenth century, these often assumed the shape of feathers, ears of wheat, or geometrical patterns of gems.

Modern combs are usually made of tortoise-shell, ivory, horn, wood, bone, metal, india rubber, celluloid, and plastics. Today, hair fashions occasionally dictate the use of ornamental combs, but they are clearly not as common as in previous eras. Interestingly enough, ornamental combs are currently undergoing a revival, as they did in the 1940s in the United States, but whether this is a passing fad or a more permanent fashion trend remains to be seen.

Modern combs are wholly manufactured by machinery rather than made by hand. The material is first cut to the general shape of the finished comb; the teeth are then cut simultaneously by circular saws mounted on the same axle and placed at the proper distance from one another. After being cut, the teeth are filed down. In the case of rubber combs, the soft rubber is pressed into molds and vulcanized to the desired degree of hardness.

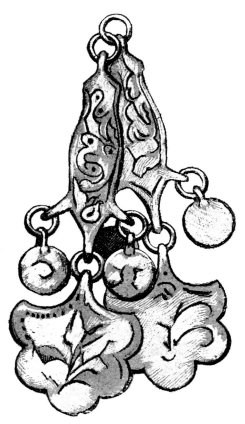

18th century Russian hair ornament. *L'Art Pour Tous, Vol. 15*

Renaissance style hair ornament. *The Workshop, Vol. 8*

19th century German silver comb. *Meyers*

Shell hair prong with gold plate head. *Montgomery*

Comb ornament; lotus flowers filled with blue and red stones, designed by O. Weber of Hanau. *The Workshop, Vol. 7*

Shell hair prongs with gold top. *Montgomery*

Hair pin. *The Workshop, 1866*

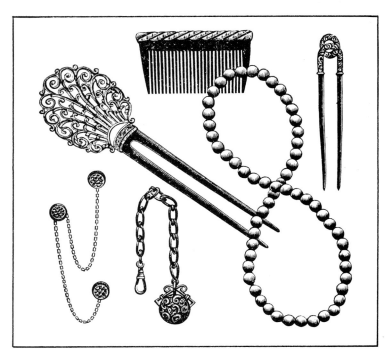

Hair pins, ornaments, and comb. *Century Magazine, 1890*

Hair Ornaments & Combs continued

Shell hair pin with silver ornament. *Montgomery*

Shell hair pin with gold ornament. *Montgomery*

Shell hair pin with silver ornament. *Montgomery*

Shell hair prongs with silver top. *Montgomery*

Hair ornament with diamonds. *Illustrated London News*

Hair pin set with brilliants. *Montgomery*

Shell hair pin with silver ornament. *Montgomery*

Shell hair pin with gold ornament. *Montgomery*

Tortoise shell hair ornament. *Montgomery*

Shell side comb with silver
scroll top. *Montgomery*

Tortoise shell hair
ornament.
Montgomery

Tortoise shell hair
ornament.
Montgomery

Hair ornament with emeralds and diamonds, designed by M.
Lemonier of Paris. *Industry of Nations*

Shell hair prongs
with silver top.
Montgomery

Shell hair pin with silver
top. *Montgomery*

Tortoise shell hair
ornament.
Montgomery

Tortoise shell hair
ornament. *Montgomery*

Medallions

A medallion is a coin-shaped piece of metal, bearing a portrait in relief on one side and often an inscription on the reverse. Often called "medals," these pieces are cast or struck into shape. Commemorative medals are conferred in honor of acts of outstanding bravery or service. Religious medals, of course, convey spiritual meaning to their owners.

The medallion, which has been a recognized art form since the Hellenistic period, reached a new height of excellence and realism in the Roman era. After a long period of decline in popularity, medallions re-emerged during the Renaissance, especially in France. This fashion was no doubt influenced by the fact that many of the Renaissance medalists were already famous as painters, sculptors, designers, and even architects. Among the noted artists whose work included the designing of medallions were Leone Leoni, Benvenuto Cellini, and Albert Durer.

Until the fifteenth century, medallions were made by casting. However, by the sixteenth century, cast medallions were superceded by die-struck medallions. Dies can be cut directly, but more often, a wax or plaster model, about four times the final size of the medallion, is reproduced as a metal electrotype. From this model, the die is cut to the proper size with the use of a reducing machine invented in the nineteenth century. Bronze or lead were originally common materials used, until the demand for more intrinsically valuable pieces led to the use of gold and silver. It is generally agreed today that the best metal for this art form is dull silver, matted or sand-blasted, because the variations of light and shade in the sculpting can best be seen in this metal's delicate shades of gray.

Medallions, virtually ignored in some parts of the world and disdained in others, enjoy their greatest popularity in France. There, this art form is considered the link between painting and sculpture—a painting in relief with the color omitted.

16th century Italian. *L'Art Pour Tous, Vol. 14*

Wedgewood-ware medallion of Thomas Bentley. *Harper's*

19th century Italian. *The Workshop, 1874*

15th century French. *L'Art Pour Tous, Vol. 15*

15th century French. *L'Art Pour Tous, Vol. 15*

19th century Italian. *The Workshop, 1874*

15th century French. *L'Art Pour Tous, Vol. 15*

15th century French. *L'Art Pour Tous, Vol. 15*

Medallions continued

15th century French. *L'Art Pour Tous, Vol. 15*

16th century Italian. *L'Art Pour Tous, Vol. 14*

16th century German. *L'Art Pour Tous, Vol. 15*

16th century German.*L'Art Pour Tous, Vol. 15*

The Stewards' jewel.
Connoisseur, Vol. 4 □

German. *The Workshop, 1871*

16th century Italian. *L'Art Pour Tous, Vol. 14*

16th century Italian. *L'Art Pour Tous. Vol. 14*

Etruscan. *L'Art Pour Tous, Vol. 31*

Medallion of Mrs. Wedgwood. *Harper's, Vol. 48*

Medallions continued

16th century German. *L'Art Pour Tous, Vol. 15*

16th century German. *L'Art Pour Tous, Vol. 15*

16th century Italian. *L'Art Pour Tous, Vol. 14*

16th century German. *L'Art Pour Tous, Vol. 15*

16th century Italian.
L'Art Pour Tous, Vol. 15

14th century Italian; portrait of a young princess of the Este family. *L'Art Pour Tous, Vol. 13*

Miscellaneous Jewelry

Man's affinity for jeweled adornments has been so keen and so universal that it is difficult to find a part of the body or an article of clothing or accessory which has not been ornamented during some era of history. Every imaginable object—from buttons to purses, from aprons to canes—has been ingeniously decorated in some era. Every likely (and, indeed, unlikely) part of the body has been enwrapped, encircled, and even perforated in the interests of ornamentation; necks, arms, legs, waists, ankles, ears, and noses have been and still are adorned with jewelry.

This section includes pictures of those pieces of jewelry which are less customary than the ones illustrated in the other sections of the book. In some cases—jeweled buttons and purses, for example—the objects were usually fashioned without jewels. Other objects are considered out of the ordinary because, like mourning jewelry or baby front pins, they were intended for only a small, specific portion of the population.

Of the objects displayed here, the jeweled button is probably the most common. Imaginatively ornamented buttons have been made of many precious and non-precious metals, as well as ivory, mother-of-pearl, amber, glass, and even disks of wood covered with silk. Usually used as fasteners for garments, buttons also serve purely decorative purposes—as pendants to necklets, as bullae (ornaments which, like amulets, have symbolic significance), and as ornaments for belts, clothing, and other decorative objects. Their shapes, varying according to their purposes, are usually in the form of spheres, hemispheres, or disks.

Greek and Roman gold ornaments, from the second century B.C. to the second century A.D.
Simple Jewelry □

Nose rings. *Bible Encyclopædia*

Child's gold front pin, engraved.
Montgomery

Byzantine jewelry from the sixth to tenth centuries. *Simple Jewelry*

Ancient Peruvian jewel. *Leslie's, Vol. 12*

Men's chain
ornament. *Sears
Catalogue*

Torque, with
illustrations of
manner of wearing it.
Harper's, Vol. 41

Silver cuff button.
Montgomery

Miscellaneous Jewelry continued

Child's gold front pin set. *Montgomery*

Revolver; men's chain ornament. *Sears Catalogue*

Gold hat pin. *Montgomery*

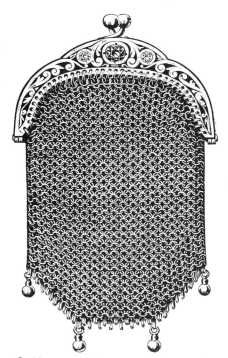

Gold purse. *Spiers*

Carved enamel. *Harper's, Vol. 21*

Gold charm for bracelet. *Spiers*

Kaffir apron. *Natural History, Africa*

Compass watch charm. *Montgomery*

Jewel of gold. *History of Furniture*

Egyptian anklets. *Terms in Art*

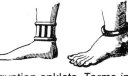

Gold cuff button with brilliant center. *Montgomery*

Chased silver cuff button. *Montgomery*

Engraved silver cuff button. *Montgomery*

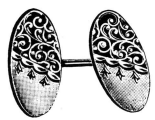

Silver enameled button. *Montgomery*

Onyx gold mourning brooch. *Montgomery*

Silver hat pin. *Montgomery*

Ladies' horse chain ornament. *Montgomery*

Gold charm with pearl. *Spiers*

Gold motor car charm. *Spiers*

Watch charm. *Montgomery*

Turquoise and pearl charm for bracelet. *Spiers*

Black mourning brooch. *Montgomery*

Onyx gold mourning brooch with pearl center. *Montgomery*

Gold mourning earring. *Montgomery*

Pearl shoe watch charm. *Montgomery*

Gold thimble. *Spiers*

Black mourning brooch pin with brilliant center. *Montgomery*

Frontlet. *Natural History, Africa*

Gold charm with sapphire center. *Spiers*

Gold charm for bracelet. *Spiers*

Miscellaneous Jewelry continued

Gold hat pin.
Sears Catalogue

Gold hat pin.
Sears Catalogue

Gold purse. *Spiers*

Silver enameled link
button. *Montgomery*

Torques and chains, for neck and waist, made by twisting gold
bars. *Leslie's, Vol. 12*

Gold mourning
earring.
Montgomery

Onyx gold mourning brooch.
Montgomery

Ladies' pearl horn chain
ornament. *Montgomery*

Mirror case of enameled crystal. *Masterpieces of
Industrial Art*

Onyx gold mourning brooch
with pearl center.
Montgomery

Gold charm for
bracelet, set with
pearls. *Spiers*

Gold purse. *Spiers*

Men's chain ornament.
Sears Catalogue

Child's gold bib pin.
Montgomery

Kaffir apron. *Natural History, Africa*

Gold enameled
locket. *Spiers*

Gold charm with
enamel pearl
center. *Spiers*

Gold thimble.
Spiers

Watch charm.
Montgomery

Watch charm.
Montgomery

Torque.
*Harper's,
Vol. 41*

Jet Victoria mourning
chain. *Montgomery*

Gold purse. *Spiers*

Kaffir apron. *Natural History, Africa*

Necklaces & Collars

Necklaces and collars—worn as personal ornaments, badges of livery, or insignias of knighthood—have been among the most common forms of jewelry adornment throughout the ages. Necklaces with beads or jewels threaded through them, or chains with suspended pendants are common to all periods of history and all geographic locations.

Torques—twisted collars of metal—have been found in the tombs of various barbaric peoples of northern Europe; British tribal chiefs wore them, as did the leaders of the earliest Saxon invaders of Britain.

Torques were probably the ancestors of livery collars, which were first introduced during the fourteenth century. Livery collars were worn to show allegiances of state; for example, Charles V of France granted the privilege of wearing such a collar to his chamberlain, Geoffrey de Belleville, in 1378. Livery collars of the king of France, of Queen Anne, and of the dukes of York and Lancaster were listed among the royal jewels in the inventory taken in the first year of Henry IV's reign. Collars have preserved their popularity as a form of decoration to this day, particularly in Europe, where special designs are used to designate particular guilds, orders of knighthood, or public offices.

Examples of necklaces, including chains with pendants or decorated metal with gold beading, have been discovered which date back as far as 1400 B.C., during Mycenaean civilization. Greek necklaces were characterized by their expertly wrought gold work, usually unadorned with other materials. Intricate fretwork and interlaced curving lines were typical not only of Greek, but also of Etruscan and Roman necklaces. During the Roman era, ropes of pearls first attained their importance in the realm of jewelry. Celtic necklaces displayed brilliant enamel coloring and repoussé gold work.

The necklaces of the Renaissance were typically large; jeweled pendants, enamel-painted metal, and heavy gold link chains predominated. During the seventeenth century, attention once more turned to ropes of pearls. After a decline in popularity during the eighteenth and early nineteenth centuries, necklaces regained their popularity—in simpler, lighter forms—and have retained it to this day.

17th century Swiss enameled silver necklace.
Simple Jewelry

Diamond and ruby necklace. *Meyers*

Silver necklace. *Simple Jewelry* □

Bulgarian.
Meyers

Etruscan. *L'Art Pour Tous, Vol. 16*

Necklaces & Collars continued

19th century German. *Meyers*

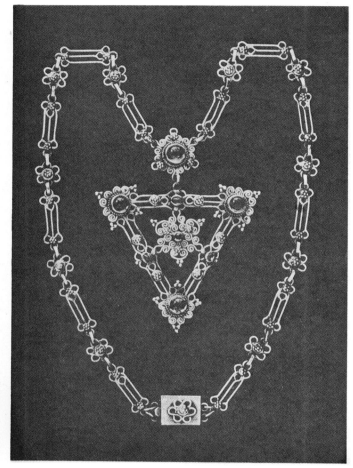

Silver necklace. *Simple Jewelry* □

Etruscan. *Leslie's, Vol. 12*

Ancient Roman. *L'Art Pour Tous, Vol. 7*

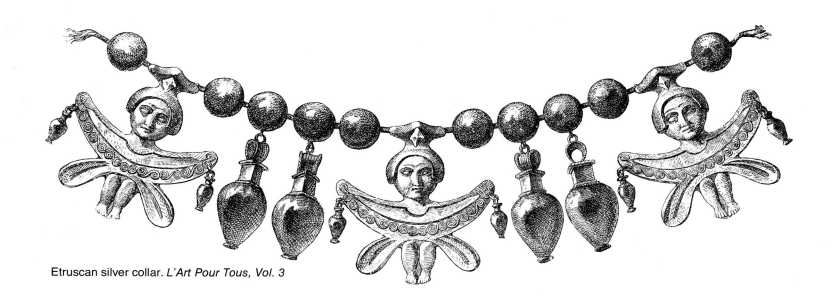

Etruscan silver collar. *L'Art Pour Tous, Vol. 3*

Ancient Roman. *L'Art Pour Tous, Vol. 16*

Egyptian. *Leslie's, Vol. 12*

Necklaces & Collars continued

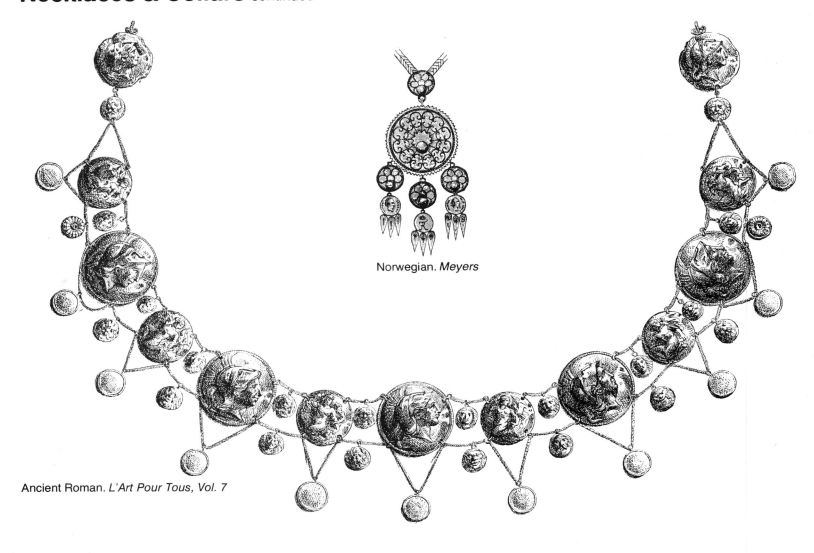

Ancient Roman. *L'Art Pour Tous, Vol. 7*

Norwegian. *Meyers*

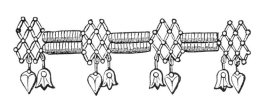

Egyptian. *Terms in Art*

Necklace of bears' claws. *Harper's, Vol. 40*

Etruscan. *L'Art Pour Tous, Vol. 2*

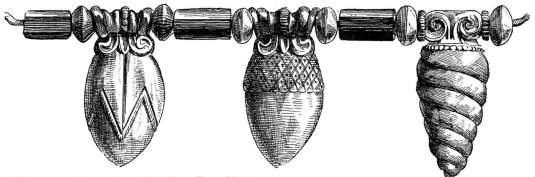

Etruscan golden collar. *L'Art Pour Tous, Vol. 2*

Etruscan golden collar. *L'Art Pour Tous, Vol. 2*

Roman collar of gold and fine beads. *L'Art Pour Tous, Vol. 2*

Etruscan. *L'Art Pour Tous, Vol. 31*

19th century English; pearl necklace with diamond center. *Spiers*

Necklaces & Collars continued

Etruscan. *L'Art Pour Tous, Vol. 16*

Etruscan. *L'Art Pour Tous, Vol. 16*

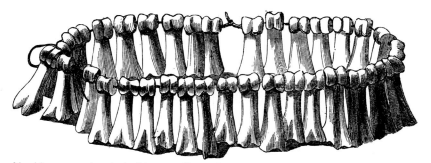

Necklace constructed of human finger-bones. *Harper's, Vol. 46*

Silver plates, decorated with coral and enamel, from 18th century Kabylia. *L'Art Pour Tous, Vol. 14*

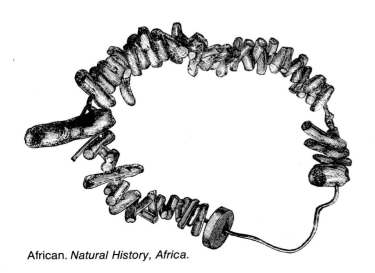

African. *Natural History, Africa.*

African. *Natural History, Africa*

Necklaces & Collars continued

Gold necklace, designed by C. Anforge of Rome.
The Workshop, 1870

Etruscan. *Meyers*

19th century English; pearl flowers and drops. *Spiers*

18th century French.
Meyers

19th century English; pearl flowers and leaves. *Spiers*

Etruscan. *L'Art Pour Tous,*
Vol. 31

Diamond necklace, designed by Bohmer & Bassenge, jewelers to the Queen. *Harper's Vol. 46*

African necklace constructed of beads and teeth. *Natural History, Africa*

Egyptian. *Terms in Art*

Silver necklace with diamonds and oriental pearls, from Vienna. *The Workshop, Vol. 7*

String of cowries. *Natural History, Africa*

Silver necklace. *Simple Jewelry* □

Necklaces & Collars continued

19th century English pearl necklace. *Spiers*

Etruscan. *L'Art Pour Tous, Vol. 31*

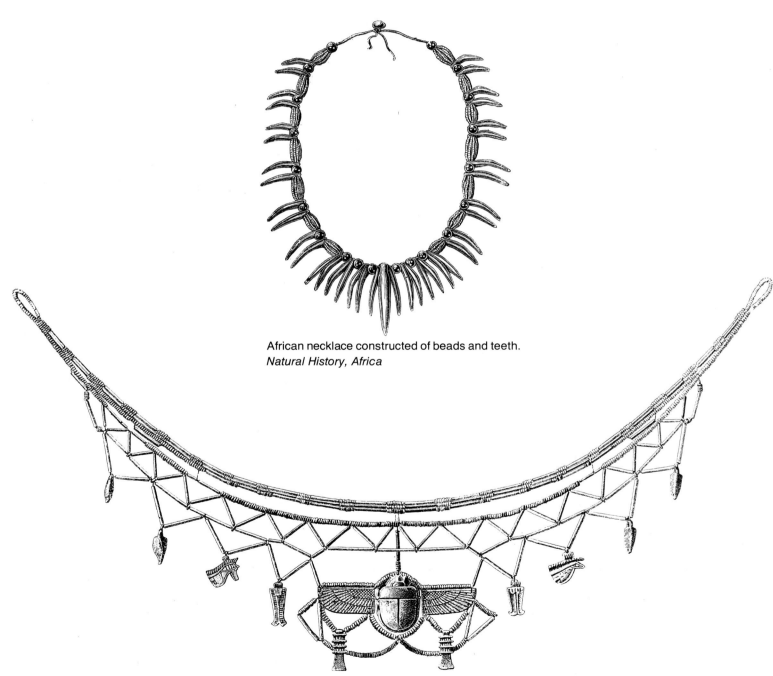

African necklace constructed of beads and teeth.
Natural History, Africa

Ancient Egyptian necklace found on a mummy. *L'Art Pour Tous, Vol. 32*

Etruscan. *L'Art Pour Tous, Vol. 31*

19th century German. *The Workshop, 1866*

19th century English; pearl flowers and leaves. *Spiers*

Egyptian. *Leslie's Vol. 12*

Necklaces & Collars continued

Bronza crotal necklace. *Century Magazine, 1890*

Silver necklace, designed by A. Ortwein of Germany. *The Workshop, 1873*

Silver necklace from Sind, India. *Indika*

Necklace from Panjab. *Harper's Vol. 21*

Etruscan. *L'Art Pour Tous, Vol. 16*

19th century Italian gold necklace. *The Workshop, 1870*

19th century German. *The Workshop, 1870*

Bronze crotal necklace. *Century Magazine, 1890*

Enameled necklace set with precious stones, designed by Watherston & Brogden of London. *Industry of Nations*

Pendants

Pendants, or hanging ornaments, are often found suspended from necklaces, but they can also be hung from bracelets, earrings, belts, and diadems. The derivation of the pendant is probably the primitive practice of wearing amulets on chains around the neck to ward off evil spirits. This practice dates from the Stone Age; the pendants, or amulets, of early times were constructed of such objects as teeth, stones, and shells.

Enormous pendants decorated with commemorative scenes were often worn by the pharaohs of ancient Egypt. Many of these scenes portray the pharaoh himself in the process of being deified. Sacred serpents, scarabs with wings, vultures, flies, falcons, and the eye of the god Horus were other common subjects of such pictorializations.

Mycenaean pendants were similar to Egyptian pendants in the subject matter they protrayed. Etruscan pendants, however, were more likely to protray human heads or figures, or simple decorative shapes such as cylinders or spirals. Typical Greek designs were similar to the Etruscan motifs, but also included the depiction of mythical figures.

Roman art included all of the characteristic designs of Egyptian, Mycenaean, Etruscan, and Greek pendants. Animal figures—especially the bull—were particularly prominent. Judging from archeological finds, however, the most common practice was to mount cameos, intaglios (figures or designs depressed below the surface of the material), and gold coins as pendants.

During the Middle Ages, pendants with religious significance predominated. These were characterized by the reliquary—a large, circular, devotional pendant—and the enameled or chased cross, portraying the dying Christ or some other religious subject. In the fourteenth century, men's pendants portrayed heraldic subjects as well, whereas women's pendants pictured sentimental scenes.

Pendant ornamented with pearls and stones. *Meyers*

Norwegian enamel pendant. *Meyers*

19th century pendant. *The Workshop, Vol. 6*

18th century French chatelaine. *L'Art Pour Tous, Vol. 32*

Steel pendant for chatelaine, designed by
Durham of London.. *Industry of Nations*

Jewel of the Lodge of the Nine Muses.
Connoisseur □

Etruscan; head of Bacchus
adorning a necklace, in the
Louvre Museum. *History of
Furniture*

Steel pendant for
chatelaine,
designed by
Durham of
London. *Industry
of Nations*

Italian pendant in gold.
The Workshop, 1869

Pendant,
designed by S.
Fink & Son. *The
Workshop, Vol. 3* □

Pendants continued

18th century French chatelaine.
L'Art Pour Tous, Vol. 32

Late 16th century German pendant.
Connoisseur, Vol. 5 □

Pendant for chatelaine,
designed by Durham
of London.
Industry of Nations

Steel pendant for
chatelaine, designed
by Durham of London..
Industry of Nations

16th century Italian pendant in gold, chased and
enameled. *History of Furniture*

Locket, manufactured by C. Ansorge of Rome. *The Workshop, Vol. 5*

16th century Spanish pendant, in the Louvre Museum. *L'Art Pour Tous, Vol. 28*

Silver pendant set with diamonds and pearl; French. *The Workshop, Vol. 5*

Gold locket set with diamonds and sapphires. *Illustrated London News*

Italian pendant in gold. *The Workshop, 1869*

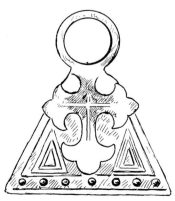

17th century Russian. *L'Art Pour Tous, Vol. 41*

Jewel of the Lodge of the Nine Muses. *Connoisseur, Vol. 4* □

Pendants continued

16th century Spanish pendant, in the
Louvre Museum. *L'Art Pour Tous, Vol. 7*

16th century Flemish pendant.
L'Art Pour Tous, Vol. 4

Italian pendant in gold.
The Workshop, 1869

The Three Grand Masters jewel. *Connoisseur, Vol. 4* □

17th century French diamond pendant. *Masterpieces of Industrial Art*

Italian pendant in gold. *The Workshop, 1869*

Locket in gold brilliants, with emeralds and pearls. *The Workshop, Vol. 8*

The John Hervey jewel. *Connoisseur, Vol. 4* □

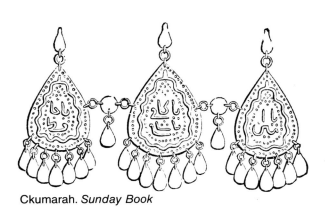

Ckumarah. *Sunday Book*

Jewel of the Lodge of the Nine Muses. *Connoisseur, Vol. 4* □

Pendants continued

Pendant. *L'Art Pour Tous, Vol. 7*

Enameled German pendant. *Meyers*

Ancient Roman pendant. *Iconographic*

19th century German. *The Workshop, 1873*

Gold locket set with diamonds and sapphires. *Illustrated London News*

19th century French pendant. *The Workshop, 1872*

Gold pendant with diamond center. *The Workshop, Vol. 7*

19th century German pendant, designed by G. Ehni of Stuttgart. *The Workshop, Vol. 6*

17th century pendant with diamonds. *Illustrated London News*

Steel pendant for chatelaine, designed by Durham of London.. *Industry of Nations .*

Silver pendant set with diamonds and pearl; French. *The Workshop, 1869*

Chatelaine, designed by A. Leroy of Paris. *The Workshop, Vol. 7*

The Alfred jewel; Anglo-Saxon. *Leslie's, Vol. 12*

19th century German. *The Workshop, Vol. 5*

Silver pendant set with brilliants and pearls; French. *The Workshop, 1872*

19th century German. *The Workshop, Vol. 5*

Steel pendant for chatelaine, designed by Durham of London.. *Industry of Nations*

16th century Spanish pendant, in the Louvre Museum. *L'Art Pour Tous, Vol.* 4

Etruscan mask pendant. *L'Art Pour Tous, Vol. 3*

Pendants continued

The first "Lesser George" jewel after its restoration; front face (left) and enameled face (right). *Connoisseur, Vol. 25* □

Etruscan pendant. *L'Art Pour Tous, Vol. 3*

French silver pendant set with diamonds and pearls. *The Workshop, Vol. 5*

16th century Flemish pendant. *L'Art Pour Tous, Vol. 4*

Roman pendant in gold. *The Workshop, 1870*

Roman pendant in gold. *The Workshop, 1870*

16th century Spanish pendant, in the Louvre Museum. *L'Art Pour Tous, Vol. 28*

Steel pendant for chatelaine, designed by Durham of London.. *Industry of Nations*

The Williams jewel. *Connoisseur, Vol. 4* □

Pendants continued

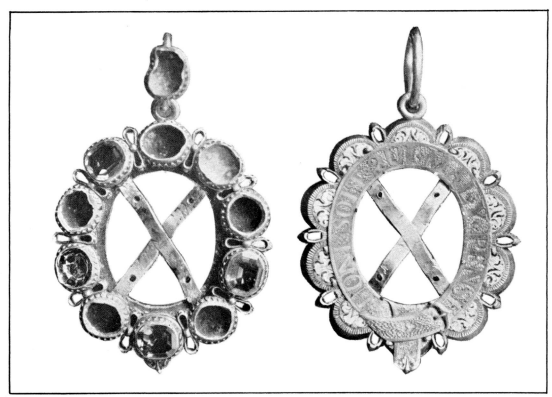

Frame of the second "Lesser George" jewel; front face (left) and enameled face (right). *Connoisseur, Vol. 25* □

French silver pendant set with diamonds and pearls. *The Workshop, Vol. 5*

Pendant. *Century Magazine, 1890.*

16th century Spanish pendant, in the Louvre Museum. *L'Art Pour Tous, Vol. 28*

German Renaissance style. *The Workshop, Vol. 8*

Pendant of the goldsmiths of Ghent, 15th century. *Terms in Art*

19th century French pendant. *The Workshop, 1872*

German. *The Workshop, Vol. 6*

19th century French
pendant. *The
Workshop, 1872*

Enameled locket
set with pearls.
*The Workshop,
Vol. 5*

Jewel of the Lodge of the Nine Muses. *Connoisseur,
Vol. 4* □

Diamond and sapphire
pendant. *Century
Magazine, 1885*

18th century French chatelaine. *L'Art Pour
Tous, Vol. 32*

Rings

Rings are generally constructed of a circular piece called a hoop, through which to slip the finger, and an enlarged upper part—called a bezel—on which the design is engraved. Within these simple limitations, however, lies an incredible variety of ornamentation, fashioned from every conceivable material, designed for wear on each and every finger. Throughout history, rings have been used for every purpose, from personal decorations to symbols of authority to murder weapons!

Archeologists have discovered the earliest examples of rings in the tombs of ancient Egypt, particularly those dating from the eighteenth to the twentieth dynasties. Evidently, the poorer classes wore rings constructed of all kinds of relatively cheap metals—silver, bronze, and copper—as well as other materials, such as glass, pottery, ivory, amber, or hard stones such as carnelian. The finest examples, belonging to the Egyptian aristocracy, were fashioned of pure gold and were massive but simple in design.

Even in Egyptian times, the signet ring, adorned with an inscription on the bezel, was quite common. Signet rings have played an important part in the culture of many countries, particularly those in which illiteracy was prevalent. In these countries, important men such as kings or ministers wore signet rings with distinguishing inscriptions upon them. By using the ring as a seal, the owner could prove the authenticity of a document or letter. In order to temporarily delegate power to a deputy, the king might entrust him with his signet ring as evidence of the deputy's true authority.

Throughout history, rings have assumed distinctive characteristics which identify them with particular civilizations. For example, Egyptian rings had oblong bezels upon which the name and title of their owners were engraved in hieroglyphic characters. In the Mycenaean period, rings characteristically had broad, flat bezels superimposed upon the hoop. Designs were incised into the gold. Stones were rarely set into the rings until late in the Mycenaean period at Aegina and Enkomi; at that time, paste decorations also appeared occasionally.

The early Greek rings had flattened bezels, with intaglio designs in the gold. This type of ring achieved the height of its beauty in the fifth and fourth centuries B.C. Signet rings also played an important role in Greek civilization. In Sparta, a law restricted the use of any metal except iron in the making of signet rings. Apparently there was no such restriction in other parts of the Hellenistic world, for magnificently crafted gold signet rings have been excavated from the tombs of Etruria and Kertch in the Bosphorus.

In the early days of the Roman empire, citizens were allowed to wear only iron rings, and even these common ornaments were forbidden to slaves. Ambassadors were the first Roman citizens permitted to wear gold rings, but only while they were engaged in official duty. Eventually senators, consuls, and other officers of state were given the privilege, then members of the armed forces, and finally all free Roman citizens. Under Justinian, the law which restricted slaves to wearing only iron or silver rings was also abolished. By the third or fourth century A.D. (the early Christian era) signet rings—especially with engraved religious symbols—were common among all levels of society.

The Celts frequently wore gold rings, judging from the large number found in their tombs. These simple rings were usually penannular in shape, fashioned of gold wire twisted into a kind of rope, or consisting of a simple gold bar, bent in an ornamental way.

In addition to its normal decorative appeal, the ring had great importance in religious, legal, commercial, and private matters throughout the Middle Ages and the Renaissance. The giving of betrothal rings, an old Roman custom, evolved into an important part of the marriage ritual, and the practice of exchanging marriage rings arose as well. Among the more common betrothal rings were the gemel or gimmal ring—constructed of two hoops fitted together—and the posy ring, so named from the "poesy" or rhyme inscribed upon it.

Memorial rings were worn to commemorate a death. Enameled in black and white, these rings were very elaborate. A common design consisted of two skeletons bent along the hoop, holding between them a coffin formed out of the bezel.

Cramp rings, prevalent during the Middle Ages,

were blessed by the king during a special service. They were supposed to ward off cramps.

Merchants wore rings engraved with individual seals or signets, which were used to seal business correspondence. In the fifteenth and sixteenth centuries, gentlemen of the aristocracy owned massive gold rings with their initials, crests, or coats of arms engraved on the bezels.

Decade rings were constructed with ten knobs along the hoop. Roman Catholics used them as they did rosaries, to say nine Ave Marias and a Pater Noster. In some cases, only nine knobs appeared on the hoop; the bezel served as the tenth.

Poison rings, with a hollow bezel used to hold the poison, descended from classical times. During the medieval period, these rings served as convenient weapons. By pressing a concealed button, the wearer activated a hollow pin containing the poison, which sprang out from the ring. A victim could thus be administered a fatal scratch while simply shaking hands.

Rings for purely decorative use were, of course, prevalent throughout all these periods. During the Renaissance, the designs of Benvenuto Cellini were especially striking. Designed of richly chased gold and decorated with caryatides or grotesque figures, they were often set with brightly colored enamel or precious gems.

Many ancient and medieval styles of rings are still worn today. These include betrothal and wedding rings, signet rings, and of course, gem-studded or engraved decorative rings. Antique rings of all types are particularly valued by modern jewelry collectors. As well as encompassing almost every previous type of ring, today's styles in jewelry include new, innovative forms, such as enormous imitation stones made of paste and set into plain silver or gold rings.

16th century Jewish betrothal rings. *Simple Jewelry* ☐

Silver puzzle ring, constructed of four bands interlocked to become a ring; modern. *Catalog of the Unusual*

Gold ring; Louvre Museum. *L'Art Pour Tous, Vol. 15*

Gold ring; Louvre Museum. *L'Art Pous Tous, Vol. 15*

German. *The Workshop, Vol. 1*

Gold ring; Louvre Museum. *L'Art Pour Tous, Vol. 15*

Rings continued

17th century ring; Louvre Museum. *L'Art Pour Tous, Vol. 7*

Gold ring with emeralds and diamonds. *Montgomery*

Gold ring set with garnet. *Meyers*

Gold signet ring. *Meyers*

Gold band ring. *Montgomery*

Roman ring of bronze. *Meyers*

Banquet ring, worn on state occasions. *Harper's, Vol. 21*

19th century English. *Spiers*

Designed by A. Ortwein in Germany. *The Workshop, 1870*

Gold ring. *Handbook of Ornament*

Art noveau ring. *Barnett* □

Etruscan. *Meyers*

Gold band ring. *Montgomery*

19th century English. *Spiers*

19th century English. *Spiers*

Gold ring with pearls, emeralds, and rubies. *Montgomery*

Ancient Egyptian signet ring. *Sunday Book*

19th century English. *Spiers*

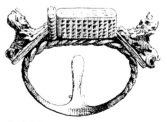

Gold ring; Louvre Museum. *L'Art Pour Tous, Vol. 15*

Egyptian seal ring. *Sunday Book*

19th century English. *Spiers*

19th century English. *Spiers*

Roman. *Meyers*

German. *The Workshop, 1871*

Gold ring with diamonds and rubies. *Montgomery*

French. *L'Art Pour Tous, Vol. 35*

Gold ring; Louvre Museum. *L'Art Pour Tous, Vol. 15*

Egyptian seal ring. *Sunday Book*

Etruscan. *Meyers*

19th century German, designed by G. Ehni of Stuttgart, Germany. *The Workshop, Vol. 1*

Egyptian. *Meyers*

Gold band ring. *Montgomery* 1032.

Etruscan. *Meyers*

13th century gold ring. *L'Art Pour Tous*

German snake ring. *The Workshop, Vol. 1*

Gold ring. *Harper's, Vol. 46*

19th century English. *Spiers*

Renaissance style. *The Workshop, 1873*

Renaissance style. *The Workshop, Vol. 6*

Renaissance style. *The Workshop, 1873*

19th century English. *Spiers*

19th century German, designed by G. Ehni of Stuttgart, Germany. *The Workshop, Vol. 1*

19th century French. *The Workshop, Vol. 5*

Rings continued

16th century gold ring.
Connoisseur, Vol. 2

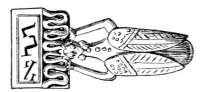

14th century Jewish ring.
Sunday Book

Egyptian seal ring.
Sunday Book

Men's gold ring with
raised initial.
Montgomery

Pink and
white
cameo ring.
Spiers

German. *Meyers*

Greek. *Meyers*

German. *Meyers*

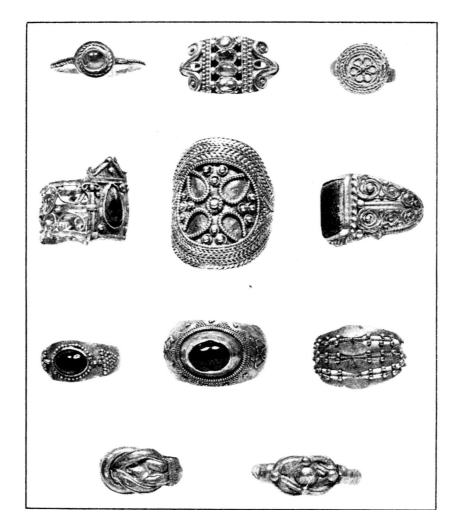

Ancient gold rings, ornamented with grain clusters and twisted wire.
Simple Jewelry

19th century
English. *Spiers*

Gold band ring.
Montgomery

Greek. *Meyers*

English. *Meyers*

German religious
ring. *Meyers*

19th century German,
designed by G. Ehni of
Stuttgart, Germany. *The
Workshop, Vol. 1*

19th century English.
Spiers

16th century Venetian. *L'Art Pour
Tous , Vol. 15*

Ancient Egyptian
signet ring.
Sunday Book

Greek. *Meyers*

Egyptian. *Meyers*

Greek snake ring.
Meyers

Gold band ring.
Montgomery

Gold ring with garnet. *The
Workshop, Vol. 6*

German. *Meyers*

Egyptian, *Meyers*

Gold ring.
Harper's, Vol. 46

Gold signet ring.
Meyers

Diamond ring.
*Illustrated London
New's*

19th century
English. *Industry
of Nations*

Designed
by S. Fink &
Son.
*Connoisseur,
Vol. 25*

Cameo ring.
Harper's, Vol. 46

19th century
English. *Spiers*

German. *The Workshop,
1871*

Gold ring
with pearl
and
diamonds.
Sears

Renaissance style. *The Workshop, 1873*

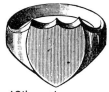

19th century
English. *Spiers*

German. *The Workshop,
1871*

Gold ring; Louvre Museum.
L'Art Pour Tous, Vol. 15

Watches

The invention of the watch, or portable timepiece, dates from the end of the fifteenth century. This innovation proceeded from the discovery that the motive power for timepieces could be produced by a coiled spring (known today as the mainspring). Because of their usefulness and convenience, watches were in great demand almost immediately after their invention.

Manufactured in Nuremberg, Germany, the earliest watches resembled small clocks with the mainsprings enclosed in boxes. Because of their globular shape, these timepieces were known as "Nuremberg eggs" or "Nuremberg live eggs." Since the "eggs" were much too large to be carried in one's pocket, they were usually hung on chains from the girdle.

The first watches were very ornate and extremely heavy. During an early stage of their development, watches began to assume a variety of peculiar shapes, such as those of pears, skulls, or crosses. During the sixteenth century, watchcases became popular, so that heavily engraved watches in the forms of octagonal jewels, purses, little books, dogs, and sea shells became a frequent sight. Those which have survived to the present day are among the best examples of the beauty of Renaissance art. Queen Elizabeth, who enjoyed receiving presents and had a special fondness for clocks, collected a number of exquisitely jeweled watches during her reign.

The flat and slightly rounded cases of seventeenth-century watches were especially suited for enameling; many beautiful examples of this type of work, especially from France, Belgium, the Netherlands, and Luxembourg, have been preserved. Two distinct forms of enamel work emerged: colored flowers painted in enamel on monochrome backgrounds; and flower and scroll designs in champleve enamel (a process in which the metal is depressed or cut and the resulting spaces are filled with enamel pastes and then fired). The most common combinations of colors was pale blue on a white background. These gold and enameled watchcases were often set with gems, particularly pearls, rubies, diamonds, and peridots.

Equally exquisite were the chatelaines, the chains from which the watches hung. Suspended from a belt at the waist, chatelaines were also used for hanging miniatures, pomanders, and etuis—ornamental cases for small articles in daily use, such as scissors, glasses, or toilet articles.

Watch parts were totally handmade until the middle of the nineteenth century, when machine methods were invented by an American manufacturing company. Naturally, production costs were cut enormously by this innovation, thus making watches available to nearly everyone at a reasonable price. Mechanical means of watchmaking also resulted in increased precision and simpler repairs, since thousands of interchangeable parts could now be manufactured at one time.

Wrist watches, a twentieth century development, have rendered the large, ornate pendant watches obsolete, but those few which can still be seen preserve the grace and beauty of previous eras.

Recent innovations in the principle of watch mechanisms have produced new developments such as the self-winding watch and the digital watch, with resulting changes in design and ornamentation. Digital watches and clocks have burst upon the timekeeping scene with amazing impact. In the near future, it is possible that digital timepieces will become so prevalent as to alter the traditional means of telling time. Children may no longer have to learn that "when the big hand is on twelve and the little hand is on seven, the time is seven o'clock." If this indeed proves to be the case, then it will be a unique instance of jewelry being not just the reflection of social change, but its instigator.

Watch back, designed by
W.H. Jackson of Clerkenwell,
England. *Industry of Nations*

Gold watch back. *Montgomery*

Chatelaine, designed by G. Huot of Paris. *The Workshop, Vol. 8*

19th century German watch back. *L'Art Pour Tous, Vol. 3*

Gold watch and chain. *Montgomery*

Gold watch back. *Montgomery*

Watch back, designed by W.H. Jackson of Clerkenwell, England. *Industry of Nations*

Watch back, designed by W.H. Jackson of Clerkenwell, England. *Industry of Nations*

Gold watch back. *Montgomery*

Watches continued

19th century German watch back. *L'Art Pour Tous, Vol. 3*

17th century Austrian. *Meyers* □

Chatelaine, designed by G. Huot of Paris. *The Workshop, Vol. 8*

Gold watch back. *Montgomery*

Watch back, designed by Jones of London. *Industry of Nations*

17th century German. *Meyers* □

Gold watch back. *Montgomery*

Gold watch back. *Montgomery*

Gold watch back. *Montgomery*

Watch back of enamel. *The Workshop, Vol. 6*

Designed by M. Patek of Geneva. *Industry of Nations*

17th century German. *Meyers* □

18th century French. *Meyers* □

Watch, manufactured by M. Patek of Geneva. *Industry of Nations*

Gold watch back. *Montgomery*

17th century German. *Meyers* □

Gold watch back. *Montgomery*

17th century German. *Meyers* □

Gold watch back. *Montgomery*

Watches continued

Gold watch back. *Montgomery*

19th century German watch back. *L'Art Pour Tous, Vol. 3*

19th century German watch back. *L'Art Pour Tous, Vol. 3*

Watch back, enameled and set with jewels, by Rotherman & Son. *Industry of Nations*

Gold watch back. *Montgomery*

19th century German watch back. *L'Art Pour Tous, Vol. 3*

Chatelaine, designed by G. Huot of Paris. *The Workshop, Vol. 8*

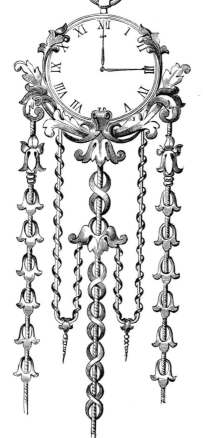

Watch, designed by Martin, Baskett, & Martin of Cheltenham, England. *Industry of Nations*

Watch back, enameled and set with jewels, designed by Rotherman & Son. *Industry of Nations*

Gold watch back.
Montgomery

Watch back of enamel; black
design on white background.
The Workshop, Vol. 5

Gold watch back. *Montgomery*

19th century German
watch back. *L'Art
Pour Tous, Vol. 3*

Gold watch back. *Montgomery*

19th century German
watch back. *L'Art Pour
Tous, Vol. 3*

Gold watch back.
Montgomery

19th century German
watch back. *L'Art Pour
Tous, Vol.3*

Gold watch and chain. *Montgomery*

Watches continued

Gold watch back. *Montgomery*

Gold watch back. *Montgomery*

Gold watch back. *Montgomery*

19th century German watch back. *L'Art Pour Tous, Vol. 3*

Designed by M. Patek of Geneva. *Industry of Nations*

Watch back, manufactured by M. Patek of Geneva. *Industry of Nations*

Gold watch back. *Montgomery*

Watch back, enameled and set with jewels, designed by Rotherman & Son. *Industry of Nations*

Gold watch back. *Montgomery*

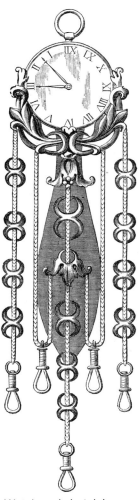

Watch and chatelaine, designed by Martin, Baskett, & Martin of Cheltenham, England. *Industry of Nations*

Gold watch back. *Montgomery*

Gold watch back. *Montgomery*

Gold watch back. *Montgomery*

Watch, hook, seal, and key of enameled gold, in the Louis XVI style. *Masterpieces of Industrial Art*

Gold watch back. *Montgomery*

Designed by M. Patek of Geneva. *Industry of Nations*

Watch back, enameled and set with jewels, designed by Rotherman & Son. *Industry of Nations*

SOURCES

BARNETT. Jewelry from the collection of Tess Forrest Barnett. Drawings by Gregory Newson.

BIBLE ENCYCLOPEDIA; full title, *The Popular and Critical Bible Encyclopaedia and Scriptural Dictionary*. Fallows, Rt. Rev. Samuel. Chicago: The Howard-Severance Company, 1901.

CATALOG OF THE UNUSUAL. Hart, Harold H. New York: Hart Publishing Company, 1973.

CENTURY DICTIONARY; full title, *The Century Dictionary and Cyclopedia* (twelve vol.). New York: The Century Company, 1889–1913.

CENTURY MAGAZINE; full title, *The Century Illustrated Monthly Magazine.* New York: The Century Company, vol. 1, 2, 3, 6, 7, 8, 9, 11, 13; individual issues 1883, 1884, 1885, 1888, 1889, 1890, 1891, 1892, 1894, 1895, 1896, 1901.

CONNOISSEUR, THE; full title, *The Connoisseur, An Illustrated Magazine for Collectors.* London: Otto Ltd., bound volumes 1–16, 21, 25, 36, 45.

HANDBOOK OF ORNAMENT, A. Meyer, Franz Sales. New York: The Architectural Book Publishing Company, no date.

HARPER's; full title, *Harper's New Monthly Magazine.* New York: Harper and Brothers, vol. 2, 3, 5, 8, 10, 16, 17, 18, 19, 20, 21, 22, 27, 30, 31, 32, 36, 37, 38, 40, 41, 42, 43, 44, 45, 46, 47, 48, 49, 50, 51, 53, 54, 56, 57, 58, 61, 64, 65, 66, 67, 68, 69, 70, 71, 74, 75, 77, 88, 89, 103.

HISTORY OF FURNITURE, A. Jacquemart, Albert. London: Reeves and Turner, no date.

ICONOGRAPHIC; full title, *Iconographic Encyclopedia.* Tucson: Omen Press, 1972.

INDIKA; full title, *The Country and People of India and Ceylon.* Hurst, John Fletcher. New York: Harper and Brothers, 1891.

INDUSTRY OF NATIONS; full title, *Chefs-D'Oeuvre of the Industrial Arts.* Burty, Phillipe. New York: D. Appleton and Company, 1869.

LAND AND BOOK; full title, *The Land and the Book: The Holyland* (two vol.). Thompson, G.H. New York: Harper and Brothers, 1869.

L'ART POUR TOUS; full title, *L'Art Pour Tous, Encyclopedie de l'Art Industriel et Decoratif.* Reiber, Emile, ed. Paris: A Morel et C.

LESLIE'S; full title, *Frank Leslie's Popular Monthly Magazine.* New York: Frank Leslie Publishing House, vol. 10, 12, 13, 14, 15, 16, 17, 21, 23, 24, 25, 26, 29, 31, 32, 34, 35, 36, 38.

ILLUSTRATED LONDON NEWS. London: George C. Leighton, vol. 48.

MEYERS; full title, *Meyers konnerlations-Lexikon.* Leipsig und Wein: Bibliographisches Institut, 1895.

MASTERPIECES OF INDUSTRIAL ART, see INDUSTRY OF NATIONS

MONTGOMERY; full title, *Montgomery Ward & Company Catalogue no. 57, Catalogue and Buyers' Guide, Spring and Summer.* Chicago: Montgomery Ward & Company, 1895.

NATURAL HISTORY; full title, *Illustrated Natural History of Man, America, Asia, and Africa.* Wood, Rev. J.G. Boston: Routledge & Sons, 1868.

ST. NICHOLAS; full title, *St. Nicholas Illustrated Magazine for Young Folks.* New York: The Century Company, vol. 1887, 1888, 1889, 1908.

SEARS CATALOGUE; full title, *The Sears, Roebuck Catalogue.* Chicago: The Sears, Roebuck Company, 1902.

SIMPLE JEWELRY; full title, *Simple Jewellery, A Practical Handbook.* Rathbone, R. New York: D. Van Nostrand Company, 1910.

SPIERS; full title, *Spier's & Pond's Catalogue.* London: Spiers & Pond's Stores, Ltd., Nov. 1903–Oct. 1904.

SUNDAY BOOK; full title, *The Pictorial Sunday Book.* Kitto, Dr. John, ed. London: The London Printing and Publishing Company, Ltd., no date.

TERMS IN ART; full title, *A Dictionary of Terms in Art.* Fairholt, F.W. London: William Glaisher, 1903.

WORKSHOP, THE; full title, *The Workshop, A Monthly Journal Devoted to Progress of the Useful Arts.* Baumer, W.I., ed. New York: E. Steiger, etc., 1868–1883.

INDEX

African, 14, 15, 25, 109, 111, 112
aigrette, 86
aiguillette, 39
Alfred jewel, 123
AMULETS, 14-15, 118
ancient jewelry, 7, 14, 15, 16, 17, 85, 97, 106
anklet, 98
apron, Kaffir, 98, 101
Arabic, 83, 85
archiepiscopal cross, 68
ARMBANDS, 16-17
Art Noveau, 18, 130
Artemis, 8
Assur-nazir-pal, 8
Assyrian, 8, 16
Austrian, 71, 136

Baroque, 116
Beltête, 72
BELTS, BUCKLES, & CLASPS, 18-21
Berawan tribe, 76
betrothal ring, 128
bezel, 128
bib pin, 101
block chain, 62
Books of Hours, 7
bracelet charm, 98, 99, 100, 101
BRACELETS, 22-33
BROOCHES & PINS, 34-55
bullae, 96
Byzantine, 9, 69, 78, 97

CAMEOS, 56-61, 78, 116, 132
Castellani, 9
Cellini, Benvenuto, 10, 129
Celtic, 9, 102, 128
Celtic cross, 68
CHAINS, 62, 67
chalcedonic minerals, 56
champleve enamel, 134
Charles I, 62
chased work, 7
chatelaine, 116, 118, 125, 127, 134
Childeric, 1, 18
chumarah, 121
cloisonné, 9
coil chain, 62
combs, see HAIR ORNAMENTS & COMBS
cramp ring, 129
cross-bow fibulae, 34
CROSSES, 68-71
crotal necklace, 114, 115
CROWNS & TIARAS, 72-75
cuff button, 97, 98, 99

De Morgan, J., 7
decade ring, 129
diadem, see CROWNS & TIARAS
dog link chain, 63
Dürer, Albrecht, 10

Early Renaissance, 10
EARRINGS, 76-85
Egyptian, 7, 14, 15, 16, 17, 22, 25, 68, 106, 112, 116, 128, 129, 130, 131, 132, 133
Enkomi, 8
Ephesus, 8
Etruscan, 8, 21, 22, 34, 42, 54, 77, 80, 81, 83, 93, 105, 106, 107, 108, 110, 112, 113, 114, 116, 124, 130, 131
etuis, 134

Ferdinand of Portugal, 6
fetter & knot, 65
fibulae, 34
filigree, 7
Flemish, 120, 125
Frampton, George J., 11
French, 10, 20, 23, 35, 37, 46, 48, 52, 53, 56, 57, 58, 59, 60, 61, 70, 77, 79, 80, 82, 84, 91, 92, 118, 119, 121, 122, 123, 126, 127, 131, 137
fretwork, 8, 102
frontlet, 99

Gemel ring, 128
Gilbert, Alfred, 11
gimmal ring, 128
granulated work, 7, 9
Great Agate of the Sainte Chappelle, 56
Greek, 8, 16, 22, 34, 56, 96, 116, 128, 132, 133
Greek cross, 68
guilloche, 8

HAIR ORNAMENTS & COMBS, 86-89
hammered work, 7
handmade jewelry, 12
hat pin, 98, 99, 100
Henry IV, 7
Hermitage, 8
Hissarlik, 8
history, 6
Hogarth, G.D., 8
Holbein, Hans, 10
Horus, 116

Imitation jewelry, 13
incised work, 7

intaglio, 116
Iona cross, 68
Irish, 49
Iron crown of Lombardy, 72
Italian, 10, 20, 21, 90, 91, 92, 93, 94, 95, 118, 119, 120, 121, 132

Jack chain, 62
Jewish ring, 132
John Hervey jewel, 121
Justinian, 5, 10, 128

Kertch, 8, 128

Ladder chain, 62
Lalique, René, 11, 116
lapidary, 10
Latin cross, 68
link chain, 62
livery collar, 102
locket, 119, 121, 122
Louis XIV, 18
Louis XV, 7
Louis XVI, 141

Maltese cross, 68
mass-production, 13
Massin, 11
MEDALLIONS, 90-95
medieval, 10
memorial ring, 128
Merovingian style, 9
Middle Ages, 18, 62, 116, 128
mirror case, 100
MISCELLANEOUS JEWELRY, 96-101
modern jewelry, 72
mourning brooch, 99, 100
mourning earring, 99
Mycenaean, 8, 102, 116, 128

NECKLACES, 102-115
niello, 10, 44
Norwegian, 20, 36, 44
nose ring, 97
Nuremburg egg, 134

Onyx, 56
open link, 62

INDEX continued

Oriental, 10, 15, 27, 31, 114

Papal cross, 68
patriarchal cross, 68
pectoral cross, 68
PENDANTS, 116-127
Persian, 17, 68
pitch chain, 62
poison ring, 129
posy ring, 128
purse, 98, 100, 101

Quartz, 56
Queen Aah-hotp, 7

Reliquary, 116
Renaissance, 10, 23, 25, 26, 30, 41, 49, 57, 58,
   60, 61, 69, 70, 77, 78, 79, 87, 126, 128, 134
repoussée, 8, 102

Richard II, 62
RINGS, 128-133
Roman, 8, 19, 34, 51, 54, 56, 62, 72, 77, 78, 79,
   80, 81, 82, 83, 84, 104, 105, 106, 107, 116,
   122, 123, 125, 130, 131
rope chain, 65
rosary, 71
Russian, 21, 31, 47, 59, 77, 81, 82, 83, 86, 119

St. Andrew's cross, 68
Sandwich Islands, 29
sardonyx, 56
scarab, 15, 116, 131
Schliemann, Heinrich, 8
shoe buckle, 18
signet ring, 128, 129
Slavic cross, 68
sources for study, 6
Spanish, 71, 119, 120, 123, 125, 126
sprocket chain, 62
Steward's jewel, 92
studded link, 62

Swiss, 102, 136, 137, 140, 141
Syrian, 29

Tau cross, 68
Teutonic style, 9, 34
thimble, 99, 101
Three Grand Masters jewel, 120
tiara, *see* CROWNS & TIARAS
Tiffany, L.C., 11
torque, 102

Vest chain, 63, 64, 65, 66, 67
Victoria and Albert Museum, 10
Victorian era, 56

WATCHES, 134-141
Williams jewel, 125
Wolfers, Phillippe, 11